EROTIC LOVE AND MARRIAGE

EROTIC LOVE AND MARRIAGE

Improving Your Sex Life and Emotional Connection

Frederick D. Mondin

ROWMAN & LITTLEFIELD
Lanham • Boulder • New York • London

Published by Rowman & Littlefield
An imprint of The Rowman & Littlefield Publishing Group, Inc.
4501 Forbes Boulevard, Suite 200, Lanham, Maryland 20706
www.rowman.com

Unit A, Whitacre Mews, 26-34 Stannary Street, London SE11 4AB

British Library Cataloguing in Publication Information Available

Library of Congress Cataloging-in-Publication Data

Names: Mondin, Frederick D., author.
Title: Erotic love and marriage : improving your sex life and emotional connection / Frederick D. Mondin.
Description: Lanham : Rowman & Littlefield, [2018] | Includes bibliographical references and index.
Identifiers: LCCN 2018019973 (print) | LCCN 2018020520 (ebook) | ISBN 9781538115350 (Electronic) | ISBN 9781538115343 (cloth : alk. paper)
Subjects: LCSH: Married people—Sexual behavior. | Sexual excitement. | Sex.
Classification: LCC HQ31 (ebook) | LCC HQ31 .M6794 2018 (print) | DDC 306.7—dc23
LC record available at https://lccn.loc.gov/2018019973

♾ ™ The paper used in this publication meets the minimum requirements of American National Standard for Information Sciences Permanence of Paper for Printed Library Materials, ANSI/NISO Z39.48-1992.

Printed in the United States of America

CONTENTS

Acknowledgments   vii

Introduction   ix

I What Interferes with Sexual Success and Pleasure   1

2 The Negative Influence of the Bible and Religion on Our
   Sexuality   19

3 The Importance of Erotic Language in Making Love   31

4 The Mechanics of Female Orgasm: Surrendering to Lust   41

5 Solo Sex: Becoming Erotic with Yourself   53

6 Understanding Male Sexuality   65

7 Marriage: Creating a Deep Sexual and Emotional Connection   85

8 How Romancing Can Deepen Your Sexual Experience   101

9 Conclusion: Breaking Free of the Negative Sexual Script
   and Living More Erotically   125

Notes   141

References   151

Index   155

About the Author   159

ACKNOWLEDGMENTS

From the inception, my partner in life and in marriage, Dr. Joan Henderson, was an enormous help to the completion of this project. She very patiently gave me superb insight and advice. Her contributions were numerous and at times poignant. Joan has been a loving partner for forty-two years. She has always complimented me and validated my abilities. Moreover, she is one of those rare people who have the ability to see clearly into the nature of things. She has been my inspiration and the love of my life. She is my best friend. Without her, this book would not have been written.

I also wish to acknowledge two of my oldest friends: Dr. Fredric and Jolynne Jones. They never stopped encouraging me to write, and their support was a constant foundation of confidence that I truly appreciate. Two of the most intelligent and positively oriented people I know, they were often my best resource to answer my questions.

I want to thank Tom McIntyre, who helped me organize several workshops, including one on sexuality. His constant suggestions and encouragement planted a seed in my psyche that germinated into this book.

Pete Kruger saved me considerable time, frustration, and agony with his computer knowledge and skills. Without his genius, this project would have been far more frustrating. A big thank-you, Pete.

I wish to thank Dr. Edward Bridges for always being such a great friend. He has been a supportive and insightful consultant on any life issue. Edward kept me laughing whenever the situation was becoming too serious and intense.

A very heartfelt thank you to Brian Feinblum of Media Connect for his very competent work on this project.

My children, Julie and Dr. Greg Mondin, have consistently been advocates for my success. I thank them both for helping me to mature.

I wish to thank Boise State University and the psychology department for giving me the opportunity to teach a difficult subject to wonderfully bright students. In my twenty-five years of teaching Human Sexuality for Boise State, the university has been the pinnacle of academic freedom.

Lastly, I want to thank my literary agent, Nancy Rosenfeld of AAA Books Unlimited, who was profoundly helpful and insightful, and whom I credit for the publication of this book. I also extend my thanks to Suzanne Staszak-Silva, executive editor of Rowman & Littlefield, my publisher.

INTRODUCTION

HOW I LEARNED ABOUT SEX

In my family, the one subject never discussed was sex. I cannot remember the word "sex" ever being mentioned, except for a few instances when I questioned the meaning of the word "sex" and was quickly rebuked. When I was sixteen years old, I questioned my father about why he had never told me about sex. He immediately became angry and responded, "Nobody appreciates what I do around here." He then walked out of the house and drove away.

With my mother, not only was the subject of sex taboo; even uttering the word would bring on her rage, since she viewed sex as something sinful and evil. Once she overheard me utter a sexual slang word, which I didn't even know the meaning of; she washed my mouth out with soap and sent me to bed without dinner. She never did tell me what the word meant or why it was so offensive. Throughout my childhood, the subject of sex remained a mystery. My peers talked about sex all the time and would mention some girl in the neighborhood that they wanted to "screw," but I had no idea what they meant.

Not until I began high school did I learn from my peers what sex was all about. While I felt a strong attraction to girls, I was afraid of them. What I really feared was my sexuality. Because of the negative messages about sex, which had been reinforced by both my parents and my church, I felt the subject was dangerous and sinful. My mother had so convinced me that sex was wrong and immoral, that when in the company of the opposite sex, I felt vulnerable and tongue-tied.

My story might sound extreme, but it is not unlike the stories I have heard from my students and clients. Here are a few of their comments:

"My first sexual encounter was disastrous! All I remember is that I felt guilty, dirty, and cheap."

"In my house we never talked about sex because my parents avoided the subject. It was as if sex did not exist, and I only learned about it from my first boyfriend."

"In the eleven years I have been married, I have never been in the bathroom with my husband, nor have I ever seen him undress in front of me. He is a good Catholic boy and does not want me to see or even touch his genitals. We have never had oral sex, and our lovemaking is always at night with the lights out and under the covers. I am sure it has never lasted more than five minutes."

"I always had an open ear for anything about sex, but all I ever heard was how naughty it was."

"I was raised with complete ignorance on the subject of sex. My first sexual education occurred when I discovered my dad's porn magazines. I stole a couple for myself and kept them hidden."

"My parents never taught me anything. I learned about sex from an older girl who seduced me, and afterward I 'experimented' around with any girl available."

"I am thirty-nine years old and have never had an orgasm, nor have I ever felt comfortable with sex."

"I like sex, but I would never masturbate; that's for sluts and whores."

"I am so tired of being rejected by my wife whenever I suggest we 'make love' that I finally have stopped asking. We have sex so infrequently that I mostly have sex with myself."

WHAT YOU WILL LEARN FROM THIS BOOK

Teaching Human Sexuality for twenty-five years has provided me with the tools to help others understand more fully about the most basic human need—to love and be loved—which I craved as a teenager but only understood as I reached adulthood. While I think anyone can benefit from the insight and knowledge in this book, the focus is primarily for the benefit of couples. I discuss the subjects of sex addiction, masturbation, female orgasm, erotica, pornography, infidelity, emotional love, and how to sustain a romantic relationship. My goal is to inspire my readers as they glean a better insight through the pages of this book.

Erotic Love and Marriage also exposes the sexual legacy that we have inherited, and which continues to this day to create and perpetuate a continuing negative sexual belief system. Much of this negative and restrictive view of sexuality has been reinforced for generations of Americans. This book will challenge the traditional ideas and beliefs that perpetuate fear, guilt, and shame—negative views that have stifled and repressed our own erotic expression. Such beliefs have taken a toll, especially in marriage, where couples restrict sexual communication and activity out of fear of doing or saying something believed to be wrong.

Western civilization has a sexual legacy inscribed by powerful men who controlled the tenets of the Church. These men feared sexuality as something so sinful that to engage in sex would be enough to condemn a man's soul to Hell. Therefore, they remained celibate while condemning the act of sex unless it was for procreation only. Their biased view also influenced their interpretation of the Bible regarding sexuality. Even today, American culture is reluctant to completely reject the sexual mores of the first one thousand years of the Christian era that are woven into our laws, our beliefs, and our American culture.[1]

The view maintained in this book describes a positive perspective on sexuality. Information on the subjects of female orgasm and male sexual functioning will make it clear how couples can improve their sexual experience. In my marriage counseling practice, I continue to have couples confess that they are not meeting each other's sexual needs. They also feel that when they do have sex, it lacks excitement. Erotic Love and Marriage will help couples improve their sexual success and pleasure by providing the tools to make their relationship more erotic and thereby increase emotional intimacy with their partner.

Unlike some countries, in America our culture does not provide us with a comprehensive sex education. While past restraints have eased since the 1950s, many people—couples included—still find it difficult to be open and frank about their sexual needs and feelings. Even to pose questions about sex can cause discomfort! Many parents today remain uncertain about what (and how much) to tell their children, and even couples who have been married for many years often find it difficult to have a frank discussion with their spouses about sex. Women fake orgasms, men worry about their sexual performance,[2] and the use of sexual slang or erotic language remains foreign to couples who maintain a low level of eroticism and inhibit sexual excitement in their relationship.

My interest in learning about human sexuality began during the early years of my academic experience. While pursuing my undergraduate degree from Whitworth University, I enrolled in a sociology course in which the professor gave the class an assignment to carefully research a subject, with all available facts included in a comprehensive report. My report was on female orgasms among married women in the United States, and I found it astounding that in 1956 the consensus was that between 85 and 95 percent of American married women were nonorgasmic. Of the 5 to 15 percent of women who had experienced orgasm, these reported instances were very infrequent. How could so many married women be unable to enjoy what men had no difficulty attaining? Sexual science has now established the information so that women today are able to be stimulated into a deep erotic state. Some women do, however, still have difficulty with lust or intense sexual desire. The answers to this problem are addressed in chapter 4: "The Mechanics of Female Orgasm: Surrendering to Lust." Subsequent chapters will focus on making your relationship more erotic and on deepening your emotional connection to your partner.

WHAT INTERFERES WITH SEXUAL SUCCESS AND PLEASURE

In 1996 the local sheriff in the small town of Emmett, Idaho, arrested three pregnant teenage girls and their boyfriends. They all were charged under Idaho's fornication law, which makes it a crime for anyone to have sex outside of marriage. It also is against the law in Idaho for anyone, even married couples, to have oral-genital contact.[1]

A mother looks out her kitchen window and sees her three-year-old daughter lying on the lawn with her pants off, masturbating and singing. The mother runs out to her yelling, "Shame, shame on you!" She grabs her daughter by the arm and starts to spank her on her bottom. The mother is frightened and angry. Her daughter is alarmed and scared. She screams as her mother takes her into the house and makes her go directly to bed.

A father hears his ten-year-old son say the word, "fuck" and is enraged. He grabs his son and shouts, "What did I hear you say? No son of mine is going to talk like that; you get into the house right now, young man." The boy is scared and runs into the house crying. The father makes him stay in his room for the rest of the day.

A woman who has been married for twenty years admits to her counselor that she is uncomfortable undressing in front of her husband and only has sex when he insists they "do it." She does not enjoy sex, never initiates it, and has lingering feelings of guilt afterward.

In Wyoming a young homosexual male is tied to a fence and beaten to death. The heterosexual boys who are responsible for this crime killed him just because he was gay.[2]

The US government spends millions of tax payers' dollars annually to support abstinence-only sex education, even though refraining from sex until after marriage does not work for most of our society.[3] School boards across the county fight over what and what not to teach regarding sexuality in health education classes for seniors.

These stories exemplify how negative teachings about sexuality are embedded in our laws, in our government, and in our lives. Psychotherapist Eric Berne coined the term "scripting" as an unconscious process that governs the way we live our lives.[4] Social scripting comes from what we read, what we hear, and what we learn from our parents, authority figures, institutions, and messages from our culture. When it comes to the subject of sexuality, many Americans are confused about what is right and wrong. They have been "scripted" with contradictory messages. This creates difficulty for couples in communicating about sex, both with each other and with their children. Lust is defined in the dictionary as "intense sexual feeling."[5] While we all experience such feelings, we have been "scripted" to believe that intense sexual feelings are sinful. Many Americans also believe that looking at pictures or videos of couples having sex is not only wrong but also unhealthy and dangerous to our morality and our mental health.

HOW THE CHURCH GAINED CONTROL OF OUR SEX LIFE

I am neither anti-Christianity nor antireligion, and my Christian faith was very helpful to me for a long period of my life. I also appreciate how helpful religion is in other people's lives, and that we find social and spiritual meaning in our faith. Just as my life experience as a Christian was extremely supportive—and even lifesaving as I developed into manhood—I recognize the same need in people of other faiths, who find spiritual meaning whether they are Muslim, Jewish, or even agnostic. Agnostics, unlike atheists, are not professed nonbelievers but are bound to live with uncertainty while ascribing to their own moral code of ethics. We also live in an imperfect world, and as members of the human race, we are by definition "flawed" individuals. Therefore, since every religious faith has its own congregation of "imperfect" people, and imperfect people administrate to them, it stands to reason that the Church—as well as all other religions—is imperfect in some of its thinking and beliefs.

To understand how America's negative sexual script evolved, and how it has influenced our sexual practices, we must examine our historic and cultural roots. America, which is mainly a Christian country, has a sexual legacy created primarily by three men: Saint Paul, Saint Augustine, and Saint Thomas Aquinas. This legacy was derived originally from Saint Paul's teachings in the New Testament and from Saint Augustine's interpretation of the Old Testament story of Adam and Eve. Augustine's teachings were further expanded by Saint Thomas Aquinas. During the Middle Ages, the Roman Catholic Church adopted the teachings of Saints Paul, Augustine, and Thomas Aquinas as its official doctrine on sexuality. The Church ruled Western civilization from the fourth to the sixteenth centuries, and its teachings became the sexual script for all Western civilization. These same teachings are present today in our approach to life, in our behaviors, in our laws, and in our approach to sexuality. These three saints have made an immense contribution to the misogyny, sexual guilt, and fear and shame with which we in America still struggle today.[6] It was Saint Thomas Aquinas who coined the term "crimes against nature."

THE INTEGRATION OF SEXUALITY AND SPIRITUALITY

Before examining the underpinnings of Western thought in depth, we must first excavate ideas from an earlier time. Archaeologists have unearthed evidence of an Egyptian story about creation that predates the biblical creation narrative in the book of Genesis by more than one thousand years.[7]

The Egyptian creation story teaches that the god Atum created the world. Atum also masturbated, and from his ejaculate was born a goddess named Tefnut and a god named Shu. Tefnut was said to have created the atmosphere under the Earth, while Shu produced the atmosphere above the Earth. When Shu and Tefnut copulated, they gave birth to a god named Geb and a goddess named Nut. Geb created the Earth; Nut created the heavens and the sky. Then Geb and Nut gave birth to Osiris and Isis, who in turn gave birth to Horus. This process of a god and a goddess having sex and giving birth to another set of deities, all of whom are responsible for creating some part of the universe, persisted until all of creation was completed.[8]

The Egyptians could only understand creation as something sexual, since the act of sex is what created life; therefore, both male and female, gods and goddesses, needed to exist for creation to take place. Their religious beliefs did not separate sex from spirituality—sex and spirituality were one, and there was no separation of the body from the spirit. Sexuality was also an integral part of their religious practices. Since the gods were sexual, sexuality was always a spiritual act blessed by the gods and made very public. There was no shame nor guilt nor embarrassment, and no concept of sin. Rather, sex took center stage of their spiritual life. They even believed that when they died, they would have sex in the afterlife. The Egyptians also had a celebration ritual for masturbation, since that was how their god Atum started creation. Punishment for any kind of sexual activity was nonexistent, as sex and the gods were inseparable, and religious rituals were both spiritual and sexual.[9]

It is important to recognize the differences between the Egyptian saga of creation and that of the Old Testament found in Genesis. In Genesis, Adam and Eve were the first two humans to populate the Earth; they were created by God and lived in a garden of paradise (the Garden of Eden). As the story goes, God told Adam and Eve not to eat the fruit from "the tree of the knowledge of good and evil." But Eve ate the fruit after the serpent, Satan in disguise, prompted her to do it. Eve's presumed relationship with the devil helped inspire the witch hunts in later centuries. When Eve offered the fruit to Adam and he also ate it, they were so ashamed that they covered their bodies and hid from God. When He discovered they had eaten the fruit, God became angry and punished them.[10] In the Jewish tradition, the Tree of Knowledge and the eating of its fruit represents the beginning of the mixture of good and evil together.

Saint Augustine taught that Adam and Eve sinned when they engaged in sexual intercourse. According to Augustine, God punished them for having sex by throwing them out of the Garden of Paradise.[11] Then God said that because of their sin, men would have to labor and work hard all their lives and women would have pain in childbirth.[12] The Church blamed Eve for the downfall of mankind. Early Christian writers wrote about her as being a libidinous temptress and a seducer of Adam, and she was condemned as sinful and evil.[13] Women were taught that it was immoral and sinful for them to ever be like Eve.

The Christian version of the story continues that Mary, the mother of Jesus, is the direct opposite of Eve.[14] Mary is described as a virgin who would never have sex and is always chaste. This teaching has been a contributing factor to the difficulty of women in receiving any measurable satisfaction or erotic pleasure during sex, since they have been taught to be the guardians of morality. An unmarried woman who loses her virginity outside of marriage is condemned as a "sister of Eve" and labeled a slut or whore for being sexual. This continuing saga has been used to support the false belief that women are the weaker gender, morally as well as physically. Women must be careful about their sexuality and their reputations so as not to share Eve's reputation as being lascivious and lustful.

Contrast the Genesis story with the Egyptian story—they are diametrically opposed in what they each say about sexuality. In the Egyptian story, creation starts with a very positive sexual script that connects sex and spirituality together.[15] In the biblical creation story, sex is sinful and separate from spirituality.[16] The Egyptian creation story gives the female an important place in the creation of the universe, which cannot be completed without goddesses. The Egyptians eventually made Isis their mother-goddess of love.[17]

In the biblical creation story, the female is not made in the image of God. Only Adam, the male, is made in His image. The female, who is created from the rib of the male, is given lesser status than her male counterpart. Genesis further states that Eve was created as a helpmate for Adam, was made to serve Adam, and was blamed for causing Adam to sin and was responsible for causing God to kick them out of the Garden of Paradise.[18]

Throughout the Christian tradition, women have not been given the same status or the same power as men. Women continue to live under the shadow of Eve's sin, which has been the underlying cause of the distrust of all women. Saint Thomas Aquinas taught that women were not as rational as men, and the Bible offers up a negative sexual position. These ancient beliefs are still in play during the twenty-first centu-

ry, evidenced today by the double standard applied to women throughout our culture.[19]

The Greeks continued the Egyptian sexual script by inheriting the
system of having gods and goddesses who were sexually active. For the
Greeks, spirituality and sexuality were integrated. Greek life was controlled by a system of gods and goddesses who participated in every
dimension of life. They had a goddess of sexual intercourse named
Aphrodite who had a son through sexual intercourse that she named
Eros.[20] Eros was the god of carnal love. When the deities we worship
are sexual themselves, it frees us from feeling guilt, shame, or general
negativity about our sexual practices. The Greeks could never do anything sexually that their gods were not doing. Being sexual was one of
the ways the Greeks pleased the gods! Nudity was also appreciated by
the Greeks. The naked body was art. Since the gods themselves went
about nude, there was no shame or embarrassment about nudity, as is
demonstrated by Greek art and sculpture. The naked body was beautiful, sensual, and enjoyable to see, and even Greek sporting events were
held in the nude. No shame was involved; no guilt felt, no fear of doing
something wrong or evil if one looked at the naked body, were it real or
a statue. Finally, it should be noted that the Greeks had no homophobia. They had no word for "homosexuality," since it was their belief that
all human beings were bisexual.[21] Prostitution was also part of their
religious practices and had full acceptance throughout the social structure of the Greek culture. Spirituality and sexuality were integrated as
one and in alignment. Being sexual was pleasing to the gods, and Aphrodite became their mother-goddess of love.[22]

The Romans inherited from the Greeks the system of sexual gods
and goddesses who participated throughout their lives. Again, spirituality and sexuality were together in worship and ritual. Sexuality, as it was
with the Egyptians and the Greeks, was a natural part of social and
spiritual life. Nudity was appreciated as beautiful, fashionable, and
wonderful to view. We know some of their sexual practices by the Latin
roots to words such as "fellatio" and "cunnilingus," which relate to oral-
genital stimulation. The male penis was considered a good-luck charm.
Archaeologists have found penis amulets that were hung around the
necks of children to protect them from evil. The penis amulet was not
only a protector of children but also of adults and even generals, who
went to war with the penis amulet attached to their chariots. The penis

was believed to be the armor of the divine force and was loved and appreciated by men, women, and children. The penis was displayed all over Rome in households and storefronts. Venus was the goddess of love and eventually became the divine mother-goddess of Rome.[23]

The Roman Empire was not without its troubles. War, slavery, taxes, economic corruption, and injustice caused great social unrest and conflict. The Christian religion, which once had been persecuted and outlawed, was rising in popularity. The Christian movement began to gain increasing power over time, and eventually Emperor Constantine made Christianity the national religion of the Roman Empire. Constantine felt that by having a national religion, Rome could be united, and a united Rome was a stronger Rome. As time elapsed, the Roman Catholic Church gained in power and control. By the fifth century, the Roman Church was in control not only of Rome but also of the entire empire. From the fourth and fifth centuries until about the fifteenth century, the Roman Catholic Church controlled most of Western civilization.[24] The system of gods and goddesses created by the Egyptians, Greeks, and Romans was replaced with a system of saints. Mary, the mother of Jesus, was named Mary, Mother of God, often shortened to "Divine Mother." It is fascinating how the Egyptian goddess Isis became the Divine Mother; was renamed by the Greeks as Aphrodite, who became the Divine Mother; and then renamed by the Romans as Venus, who also became the Divine Mother. When the Christians gained rule of Rome, the followers of the Divine Mother goddess Venus were directed to follow Mary, the new Christian Divine Mother. As a Divine Mother, is Mary not a Christian goddess?

HOW SEX WAS MADE SINFUL

During the fourth and fifth centuries, Augustine, who became a bishop and eventually a saint, started writing about sexuality. Much of what he wrote would become the foundation of the sexual teachings for Western civilization, and his writings are still part of America's sexual script. In both his preaching and his writing, Augustine condemned sexuality as sinful and impure.[25] This was not a new idea to Christianity. Saint Paul was very fearful of sexuality and taught total abstinence from sexual contact. He believed that a man should never touch a woman, but if he was too weak to control his desire, then he should marry rather than sin.[26] Saint Augustine expanded on Saint Paul's teachings by viewing sexuality as sinful. He taught that the sin of Adam and Eve in the book of Genesis was their engaging in sexual intercourse. He believed that copulation was sinful even between married couples and should be only for procreation. He went still further, teaching that since babies are born through a sinful act (sexual intercourse), they are sinful at birth. Also, because God cannot look upon sin, babies can never see the face of God or go to heaven unless they are cleansed of their sin. It was from these teachings that the concept of original sin was developed, and the sacrament of baptism became the answer to the dilemma of that sin. A baby who was baptized would be cleansed of its parents' sin and thereby able to see God if he or she should die prematurely. Like Saint Paul, Saint Augustine stayed celibate and promoted the concept of priestly celibacy. For Augustine, sexual pleasure was lust, and anyone having sex for anything other than to have children was sinning.[27]

Saint Thomas Aquinas, a thirteenth-century Roman Catholic theologian, took the teachings of Saint Augustine and Saint Paul further still. He taught that any sexual behavior—sexual thoughts, masturbation, self-stimulation, and foreplay, whether people were married or not, was sinful. Even feeling pleasure in sex was sinful. Men should plant a seed and then get out of the garden! Aquinas taught that the greatest sin was having non-genital sex with oneself or someone else, including one's wife or husband. He believed there was only one legitimate sexual position: the male on top of the female. All other positions were condemned as being too arousing and therefore sinful. He also believed that masturbation, homosexuality, and oral-genital contact were "crimes against nature."[28] At one time, almost every state in the United States used this celibate thirteenth-century Roman Catholic's terminology in their legal sections on sex crimes; some still do. In the context of criminal law, "Crimes against Nature" are usually considered oral and anal sex.

It is interesting to note that Aquinas also taught that rape, adultery, and incest were far less of a crime or sin than masturbation, homosexuality, and oral or anal sex. His reasoning was that rape, adultery, and incest could produce a baby, which partially legitimatized the sex-for-reproduction doctrine.[29] If we examine the Church's sexual script during the Middle Ages, it is clear that the restrictive teachings of the first-century Christians were adopted and reinforced and that their rules on sexuality were both restrictive and oppressive.[30] Even today, America's sexual script is officially abstinence until marriage, and the US government has invested more than two hundred million dollars of taxpayers' money to support the teaching of that doctrine. Masturbation is still a mortal sin according to the official doctrine of the Roman Catholic Church, and more than sixty million Catholics who reside in the United States are taught that birth control is sinful, since sex should be restricted to procreation.[31] All forms of oral and anal sex are sinful, as is teaching about sex, since the only legitimate sex is reserved for procreation.

Recently a student in one of my human sexuality classes asked her priest if it was true that sex was only for procreation. He said, "No, that is not true. You can have sex in marriage to strengthen your relationship." She then asked him if that was so, could she and her husband use birth control. He said, "No, because if you used birth control, you might prevent God from performing a miracle in giving you a baby and preventing Him from bringing a new life into the world!" Although an interesting rationalization, the priest did not remember official Church doctrine, which has remained unchanged since the Middle Ages: Sex is solely for procreation.

HOW THE NEGATIVE SEXUAL SCRIPT WAS MADE INTO LAW

The teaching of abstinence comes from the Bible, and both Protestant and Catholic Christianity hold to the belief that sex is to be reserved for marriage. Masturbation is sinful because it involves lust; homosexuality is sinful because the Bible condemns it; and oral-genital contact is sinful because the only rightful sex is "penis in the vagina." Again, this is validating the sex-for-reproduction-only doctrine. If you direct the penis anywhere else, it becomes a crime against nature.

According to the latest Gallup poll, 77 percent of Americans identify themselves as Christian. Pew research polls indicate that 73 percent (other pollsters indicate that more than 82 percent) identify themselves as Christian. Jews represent less than 2 percent of our population, and Muslims make up 1 percent. Currently there's a 4 percent drop in college-age youth identifying as Christian; instead they are taking on the more "pop" term of being "spiritual." Church attendance has remained in a state of fluctuation throughout history.

When we examine the laws concerning sexual practices in each of the United States, we can see how the Christian sexual script of the first century has been voted into law. Oral sex is currently illegal in Alabama, Arizona, Florida, Georgia, Idaho, Kansas, Louisiana, Massachusetts, Minnesota, Mississippi, North Carolina, Oklahoma, Oregon, Rhode Island, South Carolina, Utah, Virginia, and Washington, DC.[32]

Sex outside of marriage is illegal in Georgia, Idaho, Massachusetts, Rhode Island, Mississippi, North Carolina, South Carolina, and Virginia.[33]

Adultery is a crime in Alabama, California, Colorado, Florida, Georgia, Idaho, Illinois, Maryland, Massachusetts, Michigan, Minnesota, Mississippi, Nebraska, Nevada, New Hampshire, New York, North Carolina, Rhode Island, South Carolina, Tennessee, Utah, Virginia, West Virginia, and Wisconsin.[34]

Heterosexual anal sex is against the law, even for married couples, in the following states: Alabama, Florida, Georgia, Idaho, Louisiana, Massachusetts, Minnesota, Mississippi, Missouri, Nevada, North Carolina, Oregon, Rhode Island, South Carolina, Utah, Washington, DC, and Wyoming.[35]

In a six-to-three vote on June 23, 2003, the US Supreme Court ruled that sodomy laws (classified as "Crimes against Nature"), which include both oral and anal sex, are unconstitutional.[36] In fact, all these laws are unconstitutional, but most of the states that retain them still occasionally enforce them. In 1971 Idaho became the first state to repeal its felony sodomy law, but outrage from Mormon and Catholic leaders forced the reinstatement of the old code, and Idaho became the first state to reinstate a repealed sodomy law.[37] It is interesting to note that three Supreme Court justices ruled against making these laws unconstitutional.

The first-century Christian sexual script is still being supported today by the governing bodies of both our federal and state representatives. At last count, thirty-three states as well as Washington, DC, require mandatory teaching of abstinence until marriage in our schools.[38] Often the authorities and institutions that support abstinence are also against oral-genital contact, anal sex, comprehensive sex education, contraception, and the morning-after pill. Providing and using condoms is still controversial; sex education is censored, controlled, and limited. Homosexuality is condemned. Those who hold these views are often against women's rights and the feminist position.

When we study the sources of the negative sexual teachings we have in America, we cannot ignore politics, religion, and the interpretation of the Bible by leaders of the Christian church. Christianity, more than any other religion in America, has had the greatest negative influence on our understanding of sexuality and our feelings about sexual practices. This is not because Christianity is more negative than other religions. It is because Christianity is the religion that gained control of Western civilization and instituted its beliefs into our culture.[39] When the Puritans, Protestants, and Catholics transported Christianity to America, it became the new country's dominant religion.

Let's take a fresh look at what the Bible teaches about sex to enhance our understanding of our culture's sexual legacy and how it has perpetuated a dark effect on our sexuality.

With the advent of modern science following the fifteenth century, the Church felt threatened. Many of its beliefs and assumptions were not only being challenged but proven wrong. Galileo was arrested by the Church, and at the time of his death he was still under house arrest. To prevent his execution, he had to stop proclaiming that the Earth was not the center of the universe.[40]

The negative sexual teachings in our culture condemn masturbation and the use of condoms. Sexual information remains censored and distorted, which contributes to fear, guilt, shame, and ignorance—problems for so many people regarding their sexuality. Healthy and comprehensive sex education is a primary antidote to the negative sexual teachings that urgently need to be ameliorated so that we can move beyond the Middle Ages.

A contemporary example of comprehensive sex education and its positive effects is the Netherlands. The Dutch do not teach abstinence, believing that when children become old enough to have sex, they most likely will. They prepare their youth for sex by teaching them responsibility rather than abstinence, and the Dutch government provides free contraception and free abortion services. It is reported that the Netherlands has the lowest teen pregnancy rate per capita and the lowest abortion rate per capita of any other country in the industrialized world.[41]

Today, adherence to the negative sexual scripting continues to reverberate in our culture, and there is a contradiction between our sexual feelings and needs and how we have been sexually scripted. The hypocrisy of publicly endorsing one behavior and privately practicing its opposite is rampant. This has most recently been evidenced by many of our politicians, Protestant clergy, and Catholic priests, who practice homosexuality in private but take strong stands against gay rights in public. They profess to be Christian moralists in public, yet cheat on their wives. They vote and campaign for "pro-life" while secretly securing abortions for their mistresses. Then there are the priests who take vows of celibacy and privately are sexually active;[42] priests who act as strong spiritual moralists who are committing criminal, abusive acts against children; a Church that tells us to confess our sins while doing all it can to hide and cover up its own sin. It appears that the beliefs that have been formulated about sexuality are contrary to human nature.

It is further noteworthy how positive the sexual scripts of Egypt, Greece, and Rome were before the advent of Christianity, and how negative and fearful the sexual script became when Christianity gained control in Western culture. In 1517, when Martin Luther presented his ninety-five complaints regarding the corruption and hypocrisy of the Church, he began the Protestant Reformation. Luther realized that the upper administration of the Church preached one message in public and practiced its opposite in private. The hypocrisy of publicly endorsing and acting celibate while privately having sexual encounters became intolerable to Luther. He felt that if celibacy did not work, and he could see that it did not, then the Church should give it up. When Luther left the Church, he married a nun and taught the importance of a married clergy. He also taught that a husband and wife could engage in sex for its enjoyment and pleasure instead of merely for procreation.[43] He was very influential in starting a movement toward a more positive view of sexuality, a movement that helped break the power of the Church, which fiercely controlled both thought and sexual practices. The coming of the Renaissance, the Age of Reason, which questioned much of what the Church was teaching, and the beginning of modern science to some extent liberated sexuality from the restrictive and repressive control of both the Protestant and Catholic hierarchies. Of course this is a sweeping generalization and a broad overview to move us through history to the Victorian period.

THE VICTORIAN NEGATIVE SEXUAL SCRIPT

To further elucidate our current sexual attitudes and struggle for healthy sexuality, we need to discuss the influence of the Victorian era, dubbed a period of "moral revival," which dated from 1839, when Queen Victoria assumed the English throne, until 1901. Victorianism was a countermovement in reaction to the sexual freedom and liberation of the sixteenth and seventeenth centuries—and a movement to return to a stricter, more conservative and repressive sexual script. The teachings of the Victorian movement were predominant until 1920, but many of the sexual mores of that period had great influence in America well into the 1950s. Some examples of this power are the 1950s scripting that all women should be virgins until married, and that masturbation should be avoided as sinful and unhealthy. The influence of the Victorian era also included censoring and withholding comprehensive sex information and the belief that anything that might be sexually arousing should not be viewed or read.

Victorian thinking insinuated that men had a pathological desire for sex and were obsessed with a sexual passion unknown to women. Conversely, the well-adjusted and healthy woman had no desire for sex. During this period, Dr. William Acton authored a popular book on sex, *The Functions and Disorders of the Reproductive Organs*, which was the most widely read book of the second half of the nineteenth century. Dr. Acton claimed that most women have no sexual feeling of any kind—that their only passions are love of home, children, and domestic duties.[44] Having no sexual desire, women would refrain from seductive behavior that served only as a temptation to their men.

Women were taught to feel responsible for male morality. Therefore, women were to dress in a way that would hide their bodies from men. Victorian fashion for females included large hooped skirts, with layer after layer of undergarments, which went to the floor to hide their buttocks and legs. Blouses were to cover all flesh from the wrist up, and necklines were to be buttoned up to the chin. Men and women were to be segregated in social and public life, and sex segregation was socially enforced. There was a ban on all books judged to be obscene and pornographic. Any books with erotic content were burned and otherwise destroyed. Even many of the classics written by Shakespeare, Milton, and Dante were removed from the public and burned.[45]

MEDICINE'S CONTRIBUTION TO THE NEGATIVE SEXUAL SCRIPT

Modern medicine was just beginning to develop and, in its infancy, explained how sex, especially orgasm, was dangerous to your health. Medical doctors supported this theory, which was defended at that time by medical writers, who listed all possible symptoms of illnesses caused by masturbation and sexual intercourse. As a result, sexuality became couched in fear and paranoia. Special wire cages were made in the shape of underpants that locked around children's genitals to keep them from arousing themselves when in bed at night. Nude statutes in parks and museums were covered, and even animals had to wear a covering over their genitals. It was taught that sex was more than just a sin against God; it was also unhealthy.[46] Keeping all knowledge of sexuality from adults and children was one of the most important goals of the Victorian revolution, an attempt to return to an earlier restrictive and repressed era of history.

THE MOVEMENT TOWARD A MORE POSITIVE SEXUAL SCRIPT

The countermovement to this period was the "Roaring Twenties," the era that ushered in the women's revolt. Women organized for their right to vote, their right to protective contraception, and their right to feely expresses their sexuality. They changed women's fashion from hoopskirts to miniskirts and from buttoned-up blouses to plunging necklines. They danced the Charleston, they won the right to vote, and they developed a new interest in being sexual.[47] The pendulum was swinging sharply back toward more sexual freedom when the stock market crash of 1929 and subsequent Great Depression reversed the swing back to conservatism.

THE MOVEMENT TO RETURN TO A MORE NEGATIVE SEXUAL SCRIPT

With the start of World War II, people were frightened, and a Christian revival began. Once again there was a return to the traditional sexual script of abstinence until marriage, the evils of masturbation, sex solely for procreation, restricted access to contraception, and no comprehensive sex education. Anything sexual was censored, and ignorance was the menu of the day. People were warned about the sin of lust and God's wrath and told that anyone who broke these commandments would go directly to Hell! When men returned home at the end of World War II, the government emphasized the importance of marriage, procreation, and family. Women in the workforce were to give the men back their jobs and become homemakers, have babies, and take care of the home and their husbands.[48]

THE SEXUAL REVOLUTION FOR A MORE POSITIVE SEXUAL SCRIPT

By the end of the 1940s, women were starved for sexual information. In the 1950s more than 85 percent of married American women were unable to achieve orgasm; many did not even know how, since sexual education had been censured.[49] Americans were sexually ignorant. People feared the subject and avoided any discussion of sex, which had become shameful and embarrassing. To even mention anything regarding menstruation, pregnancy, or menopause could cause instant condemnation and social rejection.

In 1948 biologist Alfred Kinsey, PhD, of Harvard published his research survey, *Sexual Behavior in the Human Male*, which created a storm of protests and anger; the moral authorities and institutions were outraged. In 1953 Kinsey published *Sexual Behavior in the Human Female*, a highly controversial work that labeled him as a danger to society. Kinsey was fired from his professorship at the University of Illinois, his research grants were canceled, and his survey was condemned by most churches, politicians, and "righteous citizens." Kinsey had completed the first surveys of sexual practices in American,[50] which revealed a real hypocrisy in American society. In public, people seemed to be practicing what the clergy was preaching, but in private there was an astonishing rate of masturbation, sexual infidelity, and sex before marriage. Kinsey's findings exposed the controversy about what was sexually right or wrong, or even normal. Americans were talking about sex again, and the sexual debate broke out throughout the country.

By 1953 a twenty-six-year-old writer named Hugh Hefner recognized America's need for sexual liberation from the negative, restrictive, and distorted false script that had once again become standard for Americans. Hefner published the first issue of *Playboy* magazine with a nude Marilyn Monroe in the centerfold. Although the "monster moralists" were outraged, the magazine sold by the thousands.[51] America was desperate for anything sexual, and the combination of Kinsey's and Hefner's work helped launch a powerful sexual revolution—and with it, a sex industry. American society was torn between those who welcomed sexual openness, and those who feared it would destroy the country's Christian moral fiber.

THE 1960s MOVEMENT FOR POSITIVE SEXUALITY

At the beginning of the 1960s, the need for a social and sexual revolution became apparent. This was in response to the negative script of Christian tradition and the discrimination against African Americans. The moral pendulum was swinging to the left in full force. Traditional sexual values no longer worked for the vast majority of Americans. It was time for change, and the change arrived. When the FDA (Food and Drug Administration) approved the birth control pill, most sexually transmitted diseases were not life threatening. Information from Kinsey and *Playboy* magazine created a voracious interest in sex and, with it, a new challenge to free up rigid gender roles and forever alter the social mores the past generation had established. People openly expressed their frustration with the hypocrisy that had gripped the nation, and Americans felt inspired to change the negative sexual script. A social movement to explore and experiment provided the foundation for new sexual research, and the new work of Masters and Johnson, whose groundbreaking methodology used direct observation of copulating couples to support their collection of data.[52]

HISTORIC SWINGS OF THE
POSITIVE/NEGATIVE SCRIPTING

In reviewing this brief history of sexuality, we need to frame sexuality and morality as a process in which sexual scripts and moral beliefs are dynamic, not static. Beginning with the Egyptians, Greeks, and early Romans, the sexual script was positive until the advent of Christian power and the control of Western civilization, when we moved to a negative, fearful, and restrictive sexual script. Then came the Reformation, the Renaissance, the Age of Reason, and the advent of modern science, with its swing back to a more positive and free sexual script until the counterreaction—the Victorian movement and the return to negativism. But the Victorian movement led to the newfound freedom of the Roaring Twenties, countered by the Great Depression, World War II, and the traditional Christian script of negativism through the 1950s. The changes of the 1960s swung the moral pendulum back to a more positive and informed sexual script.

THE BEGINNING OF THE NEO-VICTORIAN
NEGATIVE SCRIPT

With the election of President Ronald Reagan in 1982, a new movement of repression returned to the American stage; sexual freedom was again challenged and under attack. Other social issues of the day included the false blaming of homosexuals for the AIDS epidemic, a new move against gay rights, vigorous debates of "pro-choice" versus "pro-life," and the need for a comprehensive sex educational program in our nation's schools. In addition, a new effort was launched to teach abstinence from sex until marriage and, simultaneously, a strong movement against pornography that was inspired by President Reagan. Reagan commissioned Attorney General Edwin Meese to form a committee to study the negative effects of pornography.[53] When George W. Bush was elected president, it appeared that America was again moving toward a neo-Victorian age of sexualization.[54]

Social and historical revolutions and movements are complex and multifaceted, in both etiology and outcome. Admittedly, I have taken the liberty to generalize the historical changes that have taken place.

The point here is that every action inspires an equal and opposite reaction. Sexual beliefs seem to move from more permissive to more restrictive, and then back again. This brief chronicle represents the single perspective of the author for the purpose of enhancing the reader's understanding of how our current sexual teachings have evolved over time and throughout history. Moreover, it should help the reader engage more fully and be able to attain a sharper awareness about the changing perception of sexuality as it is perceived in Western culture and, above all, in America. We have observed a continuous cycle throughout modern history about what is morally right and wrong concerning sexuality. Is it wrong to have sex outside of marriage? To use birth control? To masturbate, watch erotic movies, or swim nude? What about "doing it" on the first date? Are oral and anal sex morally correct? Can you have sex without love? What about sex as a release for tension? Mate swapping? How about a ménage à trois? As you think about these questions, ask yourself what you base your reasoning on in regard to your answers and what determines right and wrong.

2

THE NEGATIVE INFLUENCE OF THE BIBLE AND RELIGION ON OUR SEXUALITY

Jim is a solid family man with two young children and a devoted and loving wife. He is a fundamentalist Christian who prides himself in reading the Bible, the inspiration for his faith, every day. He has a strong faith and clarity about what he believes. He is a sincere man who cares about people and strives to live a "godly" life following what he believes the Bible teaches. The primary meaning in his life is to live by the "Word of God" as he interprets it from the Bible. He says he has no doubts that only through Jesus Christ can anyone be saved and get to Heaven.

Next door to Jim live Ted and Mel, who moved into their house just that week. Ted and Mel are gay and have lived together for fifteen years. They are affectionate and devoted to each other and seem well matched. They also are "out of the closet" and make no apology for their homosexual lifestyle. Both share the strong conviction that their sexuality was determined at birth.

Ted was sitting on his front steps when Jim came over to introduce himself. With a welcoming handshake he informed Ted that he was a Christian and lived by the teachings of the Church. Ted responded that he was a gay man and not a Christian. When Jim started to quote Bible verses that said homosexuality was an abomination, he had no idea that Ted knew scripture. In response, Ted pointed out that some of the verses could be misinterpreted and that Jim had misconstrued the intended meaning.

Although the Bible can be comforting and inspirational to many believers, not everyone examines what they read, and many are taught never to question its authority. An examination of the Bible's teachings about sexuality will demonstrate the lack of helpful information and the large volume of negativity about both sexuality and women.

USING THE BIBLE TO CONTROL OUR THINKING AND OUR SEXUALITY

The Church claims that the Bible is the Word of God and is God's revelation to the world. While serious problems exist with this concept, I will not attempt to discuss the scholarly work that has uncovered serious textual issues or any conceptual problems of the Bible. I will, however, address the more obvious issues of scripture. Some scriptures reflect what appears to be ancient tribal teaching, whereas others sound more like the word of man rather than an intelligent god. The real question—whether we are Jewish, Christian, Muslim, or nonbelievers—is: "What authority should Bible scripture have over our sexual lives?" Let us look at a few examples of scripture that support what Ted was attempting to show Jim.

From the Old Testament

Leviticus 18:22:[1] "You shall not lie with a man as with a woman."

This verse is constantly quoted by homophobic people who are against gay rights, gay marriage, gay anything. According to this Bible verse, homosexuality is clearly wrong. Jim had this verse memorized and had no trouble quoting it to Ted.

Leviticus 19:26–28:[2] "You shall not eat any flesh with blood in it . . . you shall not make any cuttings in your flesh . . . or tattoo any marks upon you: I am the Lord."

I don't believe the beef industry would like us to apply this verse as the truth of God! Would this not also apply to all the people who have tattoos? Where is the Church's outcry about meat and tattoos? Those church potlucks should all be vegetarian. This verse is very clear what God wants; let's apply it.

> Exodus 35:1–3:[3] "These are the things, which the Lord commanded you to do. Six days shall work be done, but on the seventh day you shall have a holy Sabbath of solemn rest to the Lord: whoever does any work on it shall be put to death; you shall kindle no fire in all your habitations on the Sabbath day."

It is also obvious what the Lord wants here. Let us put to death everyone who works on Saturday! We can do that at the same time we are executing homosexuals.

> Leviticus 20:10–13:[4] "If a man commits adultery with the wife of his neighbor, both the adulterer and the adulteress shall be put to death. If a man lies with his father's wife, both of them shall be put to death. If a man lies with his daughter-in-law, both of them shall be put to death; if a man lies with a male, as with a woman, they should be put to death."

Here it is again. The word of God says to kill adulterers and homosexuals, at least the male ones! So, if we are going to apply the word of God to our lives, why just be selective of gays?

> Leviticus 25:44–46:[5] "As for your male and female slaves whom you may have: you may buy male and female slaves from among the nations that are round about you. You may also buy from among the strangers who sojourn with you and their families that are with you."

Did you know that the Bible supports slavery? If this is the Word of God, then the Southern states did have God on their side when they formed the Confederacy in 1861!

> Deuteronomy 21:18–21:[6] "If a man has a stubborn and rebellious son who will not obey the voice of his father or the voice of his mother, and who, when they have chastened him, will not heed them, then his father and mother shall take hold of him and bring him out to the elders of the city, to the gate of the city. In addition, they shall say to the elders of the city, 'This son of ours is stubborn and rebellious; he will not obey our voice; he is a glutton and a

drunkard.' Then the men of this city shall stone him to death with stones; so, you shall put away the evil from among you."

Would you agree that this is good advice for how to handle an incorrigible teenager? Does an intelligent God think this way? If it is the Word of God, why not apply it toward teenagers, as we apply Leviticus 18:22 toward gays? Let us be consistent.

Here are a few more verses from the Bible to guide you on child rearing and discipline.

> Proverbs 13:24:[7] "He who spares the rod hates his son, but he who loves him is diligent to discipline him."

> Proverbs 22:15:[8] "Folly is bound up in the heart of a child, but the rod of discipline drives it far from him."

> Proverbs 23:13–14:[9] "Do not withhold discipline from a child; if you beat him with a rod, he will not die. If you beat him with a rod, you will save his life from Sheol."

Now we know where "spare the rod and spoil the child" came from. Does this mean that the Bible, the Word of God, supports child abuse?

> Leviticus 20:27:[10] "A man or a woman who is a medium (a psychic) or a wizard shall be put to death; they shall be stoned with stones."

Here we have the Bible telling us to kill psychic people. We all know them; they include palm readers, tarot card interpreters, and psychic readers.

> Deuteronomy 22:5:[11] "A woman shall not wear anything that pertains to a man, nor shall a man put on a woman's garment; for whoever does these things, it is an abomination to the Lord your God."

What about women wearing men's clothing, such as pantsuits and slacks?

One response to these biblical verses is that they originate from the Old Testament, which is the Old Covenant we had with God. In the Christian Bible, these verses no longer apply because Jesus Christ brought about a New Covenant with God. But, then why do so many Christians keep quoting Leviticus 18:22 against homosexuality? If these verses are the Word of God, does that mean God changed His mind when He made the New Covenant? Likewise, if these verses are not the Word of God but rather the tribal laws of ancient Israel, can we just toss out the Old Testament because it is the outdated Word of God?

From the New Testament

Now let's turn to the New Testament—according to the Christian Bible, the New Covenant we have with God.

> Colossians 3:22:[12] "Slaves, obey in everything those who are your earthly masters."

> Ephesians 6:5–7:[13] "Slaves, be obedient to those who are your earthly masters, with fear and trembling . . . rendering service with a good will as to the lord."

Since both the Old and New Testaments support slavery, it is no wonder the Southern states felt so righteous about being allowed to keep their slaves!

> 1 Corinthians 7:1–2:[14] "It is well for a man not to touch a woman, but because of the temptation to immorality, each man should have his own wife and each woman her own husband."

> 1 Corinthians 7:8–9:[15] "To the unmarried and widows I say that it is well for them to remain single as I do. However, if they cannot exercise self-control, they should marry. For it is better to marry than to be aflame with passion."

What do these passages say about women? Stay away from them, and marry them only as sexual recipients? What do these passages say about marriage? That marriage is a last resort for people who cannot manage celibacy and their sexual passions. Clearly, these passages support abstinence from sex unless one is married, but they certainly do not make marriage honorable.

1 Timothy 2:11–14: [16] "Let a woman learn in silence with all submis-
siveness. I permit no woman to teach or to have authority over men:
she is to keep silent. For Adam was formed first, then Eve: And
Adam was not deceived, but the woman was deceived and became
the transgressor."

Colossians 3:18: [17] "Wives be subject to your husbands, as is fitting in
the Lord."

1 Corinthians 14:33–35: [18] "As in all the churches of the saints, the
women should keep silence in the churches. For they are not permitted to speak, but should be subordinate as even the law says. If there
is anything they desire to know, let them ask their husbands at home.
For it is shameful for a woman to speak in church."

Is this the Word of God or Saint Paul's own bias against women?
Alternatively, is this just first century culture? These scriptures imply a
distrust of women, who are believed to be morally weak; they are the
"transgressors." There are other verses emphasizing that men should
love their wives, but that does not change the status of women as somehow less than that of a man. The men have the right to speak in church,
but the women do not? Men can have authority over women, but wom-
en cannot have authority over men? Yes, the Bible says for men to love
their wives, but they do not have to be submissive to their wives as
women have to be submissive to their husbands. Why do women have
to submit? Are men a little better than women; a little smarter than
women? Are they more rational than women? Are men stronger morally than women? Is this double standard the inspired Word of God, or do
these verses really represent Saint Paul reinforcing the cultural view of
women during his lifetime?

Many Christians, including some ministers and priests, distort scripture to support their own biased opinions. An example would be using
Leviticus 18:22 to support their own homophobia. Is God homophobic?
Does God feel that women are lesser humans than males? What does
God feel about sexuality? The truth is that the Bible really teaches
almost nothing about sexuality. We could sum up most of the biblical
information on sex in two sentences: Do not commit adultery; abstain
from sex until marriage. There is not much education in that information! What did Jesus teach about sexuality? Jesus taught just about

nothing at all. He did not seem to be interested in the subject. He never said anything about abortion or birth control. He did not address directly the subject of abstinence from sex until marriage. He never mentioned the issue of masturbation. He did not address the issue of oral or anal sex. In fact, unlike His churches today, He was not obsessed with sexual issues at all. He did seem to spend a lot of His ministry addressing hypocrisy, dishonesty, and the plight of the poor.

There is one passage in which Jesus makes a reference to "lust," but this passage has been corrupted by both the Catholic and Protestant Churches for centuries. Again, this passage has been distorted to support a sexual bias, which creates guilt about being a sexual person. Because this passage, supposedly spoken by Jesus, gets to the core of our libido, it gives the Church incredible power to make us feel guilty about our normal and natural state of being a sexual person. Guilt and fear increase church membership and income. Without fear and guilt, no churches will be built. Let us take a new look at this passage. It is sometimes referred to as the "lust" passage, but Jesus was not really talking about sex in this passage. It is found in Matthew, chapter 5, starting with verse 27. Jesus is giving one of His sermons and is quoted as saying the following:

> Matthew 5:27: [19] "You have heard that it was said, 'you shall not commit adultery.' But I say to you that everyone who looks at a woman lustfully has already committed adultery with her in his heart."

Pope John Paul II said in a sermon delivered in Saint Peter's Square and again in Philadelphia on October 8, 1980, that "adultery in the heart is committed not only because a man looks in a certain way at a woman who is not his wife . . . but precisely because he is looking at a woman that way. Even if he were to look that way at his wife, he could be committing adultery."[20] The pope suggests that being turned on by our wife's or husband's body is potentially sinful! Has he never figured out that without lust, there can be no erections? No males can perform without sexual desire. The pope's statement is worse than just hairsplitting; it is just plain ludicrous.

It is unfortunate that a traditional belief cannot be changed. The traditional interpretation of both the Protestant Church and the Roman Catholic Church was that Jesus was condemning lust as sinful, that anyone who ever has a sexual fantasy about anyone other than his or her spouse is guilty of sinning. Specifically, that person is then guilty of committing adultery in his or her heart. That makes fantasy no different from real life!

THE POWER OF LUST AS A NEGATIVE CONCEPT

In 1976 former president Jimmy Carter agreed to give an interview to *Playboy* magazine. The interview was going along well until he was asked if he was a Christian. He said he was. Then the interviewer inquired if he ever "lusted" after other women. Carter replied that he tries not to commit a deliberate sin but recognizes that the temptation may sometimes be present because he is human. "I've looked on a lot of women with lust," said Carter, "and I've committed adultery in my heart many times. This is something that God recognizes that I would do, and I have done it and God forgives me for it."[21] Why didn't Carter follow the rest of the teaching? The next verse says, "If your eye causes you to sin, pluck it out; it is better to be blind then to burn in Hell." There is nothing in this "lust passage" that says God will forgive you. The next verse does tell you what God expects you to do.

> Matthew 5:27–30:[22] "You have heard that it was said, 'You shall not commit adultery.' But I say to you that everyone who looks at a woman lustfully has already committed adultery with her in his heart. If your right eye causes you to sin, pluck it out and throw it away; it is better that you lose one of your members than that your whole body be thrown into hell. And if your right hand causes you to sin, cut it off and throw it away; it is better that you lose one of your members than that your whole body go into hell."

Poor Jimmy Carter! He was hoodwinked by the negative sexual scripting promoted by a combination of individuals, authorities, and institutions that have supported and perpetuated a negative sexual view. The negative sexual writings are designed to make us feel guilty, fearful, and ashamed about our sexuality. But why should we feel guilty about what is a natural part of our biology? The biological desire to mate is a natural part of our physiology and being. If we put this "lust" verse in context with what is before and what comes after in the text, it becomes obvious that Jesus was not talking about sex in this passage. Now look at the verse that comes before the lust verse.

> Matthew 5:21–22:[23] "You have heard that it was said to the men of old, 'You shall not kill; and whoever kills shall be liable to judgment.' But I say to you that everyone who is angry with his brother shall be liable to judgment; Whoever insults his brother shall be liable to judgment; whoever insults his brother shall be liable to the council, and whoever says, 'You fool!' Shall be liable to the hell of fire."

Essentially Jesus is saying that to get angry is no different from killing. "You shall not kill," but even if we just get angry with someone, it is the same as killing him or her! To get angry brings the same punishment as killing someone. When we get angry with someone, we have committed murder in our hearts. Look at Matthew 5:20. Jesus is speaking about the self-righteousness of the religious leaders of His time, the Scribes and the Pharisees. Jesus taught that they wore a mask of righteousness and prided themselves in how good they believed they were in the eyes of God. They also prided themselves into believing they kept all Ten Commandments. They had never killed anyone; they had not ever committed adultery. They kept all God's rules. This, they felt, made them holy men. They also believed they knew everything about God; they had all the answers to any question that might be asked about God.

Jesus exposed the fact that they are all hypocrites; He called them, "whitewashed tombs."[24] Jesus knew the human condition. He knew that no human could ever really be holy. He knew that no human could ever be righteous. When we combine all these passages into their context, we can see the obvious: It is humanly impossible not to ever get angry; it is humanly impossible to see women and not have sexual thoughts and fantasies. Jesus is teaching that it is just as impossible never to get angry or never to look lustfully at a woman as it would be for you to just pluck out your eye or cut off your arm!

Let us review: If you get angry with someone, you have murdered that person in your heart. If you have sexual thoughts about someone, you have had sex with that person and committed adultery in your heart. If you were truly able to be "holy" as a human being, you would have to remove your humanity from yourself!

Jimmy Carter should have plucked out his eye so that he could stop lusting after women! As humans, we cannot refrain from getting angry or feeling sexual desire and attraction to someone. We can never rid ourselves of our humanity, and therefore we can never be holy. If you think about it, Jesus is "pulling our leg." He is showing his sense of humor. How could anyone cut off his or her arm or pluck out an eye? No one can do that, at least not under normal circumstances. Jesus is saying you cannot be "holy" either. When it comes to humans being righteous and holy, Jesus set the bar where it is humanly impossible for anyone to attain such purity. It is a given that we will have anger and we will have lust. Jesus is not talking about sex; he is talking about what real godliness is. It is something humans really cannot attain.Humans cannot become anything like God because our very humanity disqualifies us from ever being holy. Practicing religious ritual and liturgy might make you feel good, but it does not make you holy in the eyes of God. Following all the Commandments and other "rules" might give you a sense of security, but it does not make you righteous in the eyes of God. In this passage, Jesus is teaching that true righteousness is something no human being can attain, but he is also confirming that it is normal and natural for humans to have anger and lust. He was not teaching that lust or anger is sinful. He was teaching that lust and anger were common experiences of all men. Anger and lust are normal human qualities. Jesus was not condemning anger or lust. He was teaching that they are part of our humanity. It is our humanity that keeps us from being able to be truly holy. Jesus perceives a person having lust to be normal.

Why have religious leaders taken the lust verse out of its context? Because it serves their purpose to make people feel guilty and fearful about their sexuality. It fills the churches and the offering plates; it makes people feel the need to be saved; it creates the need for confession and absolution; and it keeps the churches wealthy and powerful. The guilt and fear the Church has scripted not only helps them profit, but also benefits sexual addiction rehabilitation groups, where corporate interests profit off the fear, guilt, and shame created by the negative sexual script.

LUST, A PART OF OUR NATURAL HUMANITY

Any sexually healthy person, male or female, is going to feel sexual desire. There will be times when it will be very intense. That is the definition of "lust": intense sexual desire that results in a deep erotic state, as when we feel "horny" or erotic. Without lust, there will be no erections of the penis or the clitoris. We are all biologically hardwired to have strong and intense sexual feeling. It is the design of nature or, if you prefer, the design of God. All living things are designed to procreate. Intense sexual feelings, or lust, are part of the procreation design. Without lust, there would be sexual dysfunction. There would be no orgasms or babies.

Too often religion takes what is natural and condemns it as unnatural; it takes what is unnatural and teaches it as natural. Two examples are the false teachings of the lust verse and the teaching of celibacy. The condemnation of lust justifies not seeing nudity or not reading anything that might sexually arouse you. Even among married couples, some foreplay could be considered sinful! The Church's position on lust can justify censorship of anything sexual, even honest and accurate information about sexuality.

THE WEAKNESS OF THE BIBLE AS A MORAL AUTHORITY

The Bible is not the best text for the subject of human sexuality or gender studies. Many of the teachings in the Bible are negative about women; other teachings are outdated. If God did send a revelation into the world, it would have to enter time and place within a culture. That explains why the Old Testament was first written in Hebrew and not English. Most of the New Testament manuscripts are written in Greek, not English. They are written in these languages because of the time in which the revelation entered the world, as well as the place it entered.

Does it not stand to reason that any revelation that enters culture is going to contain some of the cultural beliefs and practices reflective of that culture? That is why we should not do what everyone so often does, including clergymen: Extract a verse that supports our own personal biases or prejudices, and quote it with authority. Out of context, we can find a verse to support almost anything.

So, let us say that not everything in the Bible which is reflective of the culture of its time, is revelation but, rather, ancient beliefs and practices of a past culture. Examples would be the Bible's support of slavery, its oppression of women, its messages of abuse toward children, and its prescription to stone people to death for any disobedience against the law. These abuses are not revelation; they are ancient culture and tribal customs. Another example is the Old Testament book of Numbers. This book has little, if any, spiritual relevance for us today. We must discriminate between what is spiritual revelation, universal for all ages, and what is limited to a specific time and place, such as first-century culture. A spiritual truth or revelation would be something applicable to every age, a truth that has universal application to life. So, what might be a spiritual truth? One example might be the verse, "Love your neighbor as you love yourself."[25]

In conclusion, we need to recognize that the Bible is not an authority on sex. To become more accepting of our erotic dimension, we must be able to see the distortion and misinformation that is often "backed up" with Bible verses and corrupted interpretations of scripture. The people who fear erotica often use the Bible as an authority to support their discomfort with sex. Jesus had little to say about sex. Most of the Bible's teachings reflect the culture of the time in which it was written. If you can recognize this, you can be free to determine what is sexually right or wrong for yourself. *You* should be the authority on your sexuality.

3

THE IMPORTANCE OF EROTIC
LANGUAGE IN MAKING LOVE

THE IMPORTANCE OF EROTIC LANGUAGE

Another product inherited from the negative sexual scripting is the camouflaging and shrouding of sexual language. We have technical and clinical language for sexual terminology, such as penis, vagina, breast, intercourse, and testicles; but when we speak with close personal friends or with our partner, we frequently substitute synonyms that are suggestive of sexual anatomy and sexual states. For penis, we might use the slang word "cock" or "dick"; "vagina," might be substituted by the word "pussy" or "cunt"; slang for breasts may be "boobs" or "tits"; engaging in intercourse might be referred to as "screwing" or "fucking" or "making love"; and "nuts" or "balls" is the vernacular for testicles. This kind of sexually-charged jargon is sometimes known as "street" or "locker-room" talk, but it can also stimulate erotic feelings and sexual passion between partners.

During my practice as a licensed marriage counselor, I have counseled many couples, but two specific cases illustrate more clearly the importance of erotic language. In the first case, the wife had a problem reaching orgasm during intercourse with her husband unless he resorted to "dirty talk" while they were having sex. In this case, the husband was a devout Catholic who felt that street language was disrespectful to his wife and a sin. He didn't want to speak to any woman like that, let alone his own wife! But if he didn't use sexually charged language in bed, she complained, and he became upset with her for insisting when she knew he considered it a sin. Sometimes she purposely got him intoxicated before sex so that he would talk "dirty" to her, which stimulated her to orgasm. The next morning, he would be angry with her for manipulating him against his wishes.

The second case was just the opposite. The husband liked "dirty talk" during foreplay and intercourse, but his wife felt like a whore when he addressed her that way. People who have a problem with erotic language have usually been influenced into thinking "lust is sinful" and should therefore be avoided.

THE MADONNA-WHORE COMPLEX

The above case scenarios illustrate some of the characteristics of the "Madonna-Whore Complex." The contrast between Eve and Mary, the "Mother of God," established the dichotomy of women as either whores or saints.[1] Though usually a male problem, a form of the complex plays out similarly for women. In short, the man (or woman) feels so much love and respect for his partner that he cannot take pleasure from her; he can only give her pleasure. His sole focus is attending to his partner to make certain she is pleased and satisfied in their sexual coupling. In restraining his own sexual emotions, he has difficulty letting himself desire his "Madonna" wife. But when having sex with a woman he neither loves nor respects, he is able to visualize her as a sex object for his personal pleasure and allows himself to become deeply erotic so that he can take all the enjoyment he can from her body. She becomes his "whore" as opposed to his wife, the "Madonna." This explains why some men can love their wives while simultaneously craving sex from someone else. Sadly, when many women get married and begin having children, they begin to act like the Madonna!

Other women can have sex with their husbands without reaching orgasm, or they work hard just to have a "weak" climax. With some stranger they hardly know, they are able to "let it all out," so their sex outside of marriage is more exciting than they ever experienced with their husbands. Why is this so? Their husbands usually are controlling males who posture more like a parent than a spouse, and the wives experience them as "father figures." Is good sex possible with someone who is parental? Could it reveal a latent subconscious feeling about incest taboos? A sexual partner should be an erotic animal, not a parent! If your partner inhibits the use of erotic language, he may be stuck in the parent ego state. The parent ego state goes hand in hand with maintaining the negative sexual script that is rooted in the first century. Sex that originates from a sense of duty is never as good as sex that comes from intense sexual feelings, or lust.[2]

The woman who did not want her husband to use dirty language when they had sex exemplifies the "mother object" versus the "sex object." If we stop thinking of sexual slang as dirty and begin thinking of it as erotic communication that is decoding our desires and our partner's passion, then "dirty talk" will enrich the sexual relationship and sexual pleasure. Where did we get the idea that erotic language is dirty? If we look deeper for the answer, we find it is dirty simply because it is erotic. Those who promote the negative sexual script feel that propriety should be maintained when having sex, and that our sexual feelings should be controlled. If you are female, society frowns when "good girls" use words like "whore" or "slut" because that is how "bad girls" speak. Women should not become like Eve; they should have sex without becoming libidinous. The woman who becomes comfortable with the "bad girl," or "whore," parts of her anatomy that are linked to the libido receives the message that her actions might become sexually addictive and ruin her life! This is the message of "monster moralists," who create sexual negativity and erotic fear and are responsible for sexual repression and frustration. That it is shameful to be sexual with our mate was the message imparted by Saints Paul, Augustine, and Thomas Aquinas. The idea that it's a sin to feel erotic pleasure with your mate has been perpetuated by our conventional culture.

MAKING EROTICA

What is "making erotica" versus "making love"? Love is more of an emotion than it is physical, and it contains deep levels of empathy, sensitivity, and affectionate devotion. The subject of emotional love will be addressed more fully in chapters 7 and 8. It is important for partners to appreciate both the concept and the value of "making erotica," because love alone is not enough for any meaningful, pleasurable orgasmic sex. Nor is love primary to the successful peak of pleasure in a sexual relationship. Most important is that couples learn how to immerse themselves in a deep erotic state, both psychologically and physiologically. Consequently, "fucking" may be a more helpful symbol than "making love," and creating sexual tension and passion is what good sex is about.

The well-known sexual research team of Masters and Johnson became famous for their unique work in researching the process of human sexual response and the treatment of sexual dysfunction. What made their work groundbreaking was the methodology of their research. They were the first to use direct observation of couples having sexual intercourse, and they observed more than ten thousand cycles of intercourse. The results of their research were a revelation on the physiological responses in couples during sexual intercourse that culminated in orgasm.[3] They also studied couples with sexual dysfunction and developed a new approach to sex therapy that had an 80 percent success rate. The work of Masters and Johnson became known as "The Four Phase Sexual Response Cycle."[4] The first phase, "The Excitement Phase," is one of the most important steps of the four-cycle approach. In stage one the couple is guided on how to prepare for sex. This requires both psychological and physiological changes in both partners, which is the buildup of sexual excitement or sexual tension. Murray S. Davis, the author of Smut: Erotic Reality/Obscene Ideology, coined terminology to describe the shift that needs to evolve from the state in which we feel no sexual desire to the state in which our excitement has peaked. She uses the phrase "everyday reality" in contrast to "erotic reality."[5] When we are in a state of everyday reality, we don't feel very sexual or erotic. In daily reality we are focusing on responsible life maintenance, which constitutes daily chores such as jobs, childcare, housekeeping, home maintenance, household errands, or meeting social and family obligations. The actual act of intercourse should never begin until the couple has completed the process of the first stage.

Stage two begins with sexual intercourse. In erotic reality, our mind should be focused on sexual pleasure, concentrating on the sexual sensations being stimulated. Our effort is to increase sexual tension and enjoy erotic pleasure. This is the stage where a couple gets into what is popularly called "foreplay." We are literally making or creating erotica. We are doing things that stimulate the erogenous zones on each other's anatomy. We are going deep into our libido and surrendering to lust. Psychologically, we are giving into our desire to mate. Whatever one says, it should be erotic language. Whatever one does, it should increase sexual tension in oneself and in one's partner.

GETTING SEXUALLY EXCITED

Imagine the excitement stage as being on a scale of 1 to 10, with 10 being close to reaching orgasm. When the male comes to the female, he usually has already reached stage 6 or 7, whereas his female partner is often somewhere between 1 and 3. As the couple begins to shift from daily reality to erotic reality, the male escalates to 9. He wants to enter and start stroking, but his female partner is only at 6. If she prematurely opens the gate before she is close to sexual tension, she probably will not have an orgasm because her partner will "come" and release before she is able to climax; she'll be left unfulfilled and unsatisfied.

Most important in the excitement phase is stimulating the physical changes within our bodies, which prepares us so that we can perform adequately and experience maximum pleasure and enjoyment. To illustrate, let us describe what happens in a female when she starts to kiss and "make out" with her lover. As she is being kissed and caressed, her eyes begin to dilate, her earlobes fill with blood, and her lips swell as her mouth fills with saliva. Simultaneously, the nipples on her breasts become erect and blood begins moving into her vaginal area. Whenever there is engorgement of blood, the heat of the vagina reaches a temperature between 104°F and 107°F and the vaginal lips swell with blood. The lining of the vaginal walls also swells with blood, and a clear slippery fluid begins to appear as the woman becomes increasingly aroused. Then the sphincter muscle of the outer third of her vagina becomes relaxed for easy penetration.

But imagine what would happen if a young woman's parents suddenly entered the front door, or a woman's husband unexpectedly arrived home, or a cop shined a flashlight through the car window, or a couple's child started to cry. The woman's adrenal glands would secrete adrenalin into her blood stream, and the following changes would take place. She would open her eyes, the blood would move out of her earlobes and lips, the pores in her mouth would close and dry up her mouth, the nipples on her breasts would become lax; the engorgement of blood in her pelvic area would recede until she was dry, which would cause the vaginal lips to shrink and the sphincter muscle in the outer portion of her vagina to contract shut, making penetration difficult. A male also experiences physiological changes similar to the female's, but instead of vaginal lubrication, he has an erection; and when caught in the act, the erection deflates.

For both men and women, it takes more than just an agreement to have satisfying sex. They need the increase of sexual arousal that causes physical changes to prepare them for sexual intercourse and orgasm. To have pleasurable feelings and orgasm, each partner needs a buildup of sexual tension almost to the point of "coming."

Besides physical stimulation and arousal, there also is a need for psychological preparation. Kaplan's sexual response model is different from Masters and Johnson's. Kaplan has a three-stage model that begins with desire, then excitement, and then orgasm.[6] How can we have enjoyment and sexual pleasure without desire? We could explain lack of desire as "being stuck in daily reality and unable to make the transition into erotic reality." Couples can also create a desirable atmosphere that gets them into a sexual mood.

Learning how to get into a deep erotic state can make for a strong deep bond and a meaningful sexual experience. Great sex enriches a marriage as it does any relationship.

SHIFTING FROM DAILY REALITY TO EROTIC REALITY

John and Mary have been married for seven years and have two children: a boy who is five years old and a three-year-old girl. Both John and Mary have MBA degrees and hold managerial positions at large companies across town from each other. Mary drives a new Volvo and John drives a new BMW. Their routine is as follows: Mary gets up in the morning at 6:00 a.m., puts the coffee on, and showers to get ready for work. John, a "new age sensitive male," gets up and wakes the kids for breakfast. After he has fed them breakfast, Mary dresses the children. John drives their son to preschool on the way to work, and Mary drops their daughter off at nursery school before heading to her job.

Let us follow Mary's day. She arrives at work around 8:15 a.m., and her secretary hands her messages that await her immediate attention. She remembers an important meeting scheduled at 8:30 that morning, where she needs to present her marketing goals and objectives to her boss and colleagues.

Bill is one of Mary's colleagues; he competed with her last year for the advancement she ended up getting. He is still very angry and feels he should have been offered the position instead of Mary. Bill is determined to make her look bad in front of her boss. When Mary starts to present her project, Bill immediately steps in to tear it apart. Finally it's lunchtime, and the meeting adjourns until 2:00 p.m. Mary's secretary hands her additional messages about phone calls she needs to return; she selects the most important ones and calls them back. Now it is noontime, and she has an important lunch meeting with a potential high-end client. She phones to let him know she's on her way. She gets to the meeting late, but the meeting goes well, and they set up another time to meet. When the two o'clock meeting resumes, Bill continues to pick her apart with questions she cannot answer without additional research. They all agree to reconvene the following morning; Mary assures everyone that she'll do the necessary research and be prepared to respond to Bill's questions.

At five o'clock she leaves her office to pick up her daughter at nursery school before heading home. By the time she arrives home, John is already there, and Mary asks him to keep the children occupied while she makes dinner. At the dinner table, neither John nor Mary can speak because the kids do all the talking. Before long, the children are fighting, making faces, and throwing food at each other. Despite the crying and yelling, they somehow get through dinner. Mary informs John that she has research to do and will be on the computer. She asks if he would mind reading to the children and giving them their bath. He agrees, and Mary gets to work so that she'll be ready for the morning meeting. When it's time for the children's bath, they protest loudly that only Mommy can give them their bath, not Daddy. Both kids have a meltdown, screaming for Mommy! Mary comes out and agrees to bathe them and get them ready for bed. Then she gets back to work for the morning's meeting.

Meanwhile, John has been watching television and drinking beer. Just after ten o'clock he goes into Mary's home office to find out how much longer she plans to work, since he wants to get to bed. She says about twenty minutes, and John gets into bed and reads while waiting for Mary. When Mary comes into the bedroom thirty minutes later, John notices how tired and stressed she looks. He asks what's wrong, and she tells him about the meeting and about Bill's hostility. John reacts immediately:

"You don't have to take any shit from him. Tell him to go fuck himself." Mary gets angry and complains that he's making the situation worse, not better. John's response is patronizing: "If you can't take the heat, then get out of the kitchen."

"What do you mean?" asks Mary. "That I quit my job? Do you expect us to make our house and car payments on your salary alone? You're such an asshole!" John calls her a bitch, and she climbs into bed and turns off the light. They lie quietly in the dark quietly, their backs toward each other, until finally John rolls over to speak with her.

"Do you want to make love?" he asks.

"No, I am too tired," she responds.

John: "You are always too tired. You never want to have sex."

Mary: "That's not true. We had sex Friday night and Saturday night, and you're the one who said you were too tired on Sunday."

John: "You never want to do it, and you keep me sexually frustrated."

Mary: "You are such an asshole."

The conversation ends abruptly, with neither wanting to make another move.

Let us consider a different scenario for the same story. Mary comes into the bedroom looking tired and stressed, and John asks her how she's feeling. She replies, "It's Bill. In the meeting today, he just kept picking me apart."

John: "That must really be difficult, having to deal with his hostilities in front of the boss and your colleagues."

Mary: "It was starting to get to me, but I think I am ready for him for tomorrow."

John: "Let me help you. When you get up in the morning, just get out of here; I'll get the kids up and get them off to school. I want to help because you have your hands full and do plenty for all of us. I think you're amazing, and I'm a lucky guy to have you as my partner and the mother of our children."

Then John gets up, gets a jar of body lotion from the top of the dresser, and starts to massage Mary's feet. At first she resists, but as he continues she finally gives in. Then he massages her legs, her back and neck, and her arms and hands. There is nothing sexual about John's motives. He only wants to help Mary relax and to be comforting.
"Mmm," responds Mary. "That feels so good. You're wonderful. "How did I get so lucky to ever find you? You are such a love!"
John finishes the massage, switches off the light, and they lie side by side in the quiet dark. Mary turns toward John, lays her hand on his penis as she slowly and lovingly strokes him. Softly, she whispers in his ear, "John, let's make love." They come together for nearly an hour before both collapse in each other's arms and fall asleep.
In the first scenario, John did nothing to help ease Mary out of her everyday reality. The second scenario is dramatically different, as are its results. Sometimes, all it takes are some comforting words and actions, a little empathy to help shift the mood to the excitement phase. Spending a little time talking with your spouse about sexual feelings or sharing sexual fantasies can also be a turn-on. Watching a portion of an erotic movie or reading an explicit sexual passage from a novel also can trump daily reality and move you into erotic reality. So can exercising together and then relaxing while talking about all the things that are right about your relationship—all the things you find attractive about your partner. This ultimately will trigger the emotional response that will get you into the mood and emotionally connected. Or you might come right out and say, "I really want to have sex with you tonight."

4

THE MECHANICS OF FEMALE ORGASM

Surrendering to Lust

FAKING ORGASMS

The one question women don't want to hear after sex is the proverbial "Did you come?" Why should a woman be interrogated after sex? I can't think of any male who would want to be questioned about his performance, such as "Couldn't you last longer?" or "What took you so long?" or "Why didn't you come?" Imagine a woman with two recordings on her iPhone—one of an auditorium filled with people who are applauding; the second of an audience that is booing. How she felt about her partner's ability at foreplay would determine which recording she played to him.

The question "Did you come?" begs the woman to lie. Whether she enjoyed the sexual experience or not is all but discounted, even canceled out, if she dares to tell the truth and say, "No, I didn't." It is much easier to just fake it than tell the truth! For far too many males, if their partner fails to climax, it's like a solo concert with no applause at the end. One could argue that women fake orgasms because males are so performance-focused during sex that their egos will be wounded if their female partner doesn't say that she came.

Many women grow up learning to be pleasers; they are socially conditioned to focus on their spouse rather than on themselves. They want to make their partner feel good and not hurt his feelings. They also don't want to be judged as sexually inadequate. "Did you come?" is no different than a parent asking, "Did you brush your teeth?" There are times when women are content simply to satisfy their partner. They also enjoy the closeness they feel when having sex. While they enjoy having an orgasm, they don't feel it necessary to come every time they are sexual with their partner. What some men don't understand is that women enjoy sex whether they have an orgasm or not.

Surveys indicate that 60 percent of women have faked orgasms, and that 75 percent of those women have faked orgasms more than fifty times. Nearly 10 percent admit to faking orgasms all the time! The data is much lower for males, with only about 17 percent of males faking orgasms. Some men will say they came when they lost their erection during sex, while other men—even some women—fake orgasm just to get sex over with.[1]

Faking orgasms creates issues for both partners. It is a form of counterfeiting that sets up a dualism of the truth versus fiction. The truth is that you didn't come, and the fiction is that you said you did, which is untrue. How does this deception affect your self-esteem, and how does it impact your partner? Once you start this falsehood, you must continue the lie, which emotionally disconnects you from your partner. True emotional intimacy is a connection between you and your partner's inner private self. Conversely, hiding how we honestly feel prevents a deeper emotional intimacy while maintaining the tension of not being fully connected. This is psychologically unhealthy for the relationship.

Orgasms are determined by at least two factors, the first having to do with you and the second with your partner. Do you usually have difficulty reaching orgasm with a partner? If your answer is affirmative, then you need additional sex education. If you have little difficulty coming during masturbation but always do with a partner, then the problem may rest with you and not your partner. If, on the other hand, you have a history of being able to reach full satisfaction with a partner but have difficulty with your current partner, you need to examine your relationship. How do you feel about your partner? Do you find him physically attractive? Is there anything about your paramour's technique or style that is a turn-off? Are there conflicts in the nonsexual dimension of your relationship that may be spilling into your sexual relationship?

How much do you personally know about the process of having orgasms? What inhibitions or sexual blocks get in the way for you? Based on what you know, how would you rate your orgasmic IQ? There is no real need to fake an orgasm. Sexual science has provided the information that enables everyone to experience orgasm. Although no books have been written to instruct men on the "art" of achieving orgasm, many books are on the market for women because they have the most difficulty attaining orgasm. The reason is the way women have been socially conditioned by the American negative sexual script. In some countries women have little to no difficulty. On the Polynesian island of Mangaia, women are multiorgasmic and come with little difficulty, but American men are less knowledgeable about how to make love with a woman, even if they consider themselves a "sexpert." To make this important discrimination, you need to do some serious soul searching and ask yourself how much is really you and how much is your partner? Then it would be healthy to honestly respond that you did not "come" but that you are "working on it." If the problem is your partner, you need to be honest and tell him that you need to talk about why you're having difficulty coming with him.

The truth is, an orgasm cannot be faked. Any man who knows about female orgasms can tell a real one from a fake. All female orgasms are the same—not in intensity but in their muscle response. The female orgasm, like the male orgasm, is spontaneous pelvic contractions, and you can feel these contractions. Each contraction brings a surge of pleasure and a release of sexual tension. You can't fake that any more than you could pass off a counterfeit one-hundred-dollar bill to a banker. The process of having an orgasm is simply building sexual tension to a point of involuntary release of tension. What you need to examine and become aware of is what inhibits your creation of sexual tension, and what blocks your ability to surrender to building sexual tension.

From what I have learned in more than forty years of providing relationship counseling for couples, all couples have sexual issues of one kind or another, as does most every individual. By addressing your sexual issues and self-educating, you will become sexually competent. There will be no need to ever fake an orgasm, as you will learn how to achieve orgasm without much effort.

Besides dealing with gender discrimination, women must struggle with a long history of negative conditioning about their sexuality. The negative messages that women receive from social conditioning in early childhood makes one wonder why any female would want anything to do with sex. There is almost universal agreement that a woman's sexual response pattern and her ability to achieve (or not achieve) orgasm is largely psychological. An exception to the rule would be a woman going through menopause or other hormone issues.[2]

What is true for almost everyone in our culture is the limited access to comprehensive sex education, which makes it difficult for parents, teachers, and students to find accurate and appropriate information and rational discussion about sexuality. Most parents feel uncomfortable about how much information to give children about sex, and age-appropriate books are too often missing from the shelves of school libraries. Although boys can talk to other boys about sex and find answers in porn magazines, girls are more inhibited to talk about sex because they've been taught that sex is "naughty" and "dirty," and that only "bad" girls have sex. Instead, most girls fantasize that one day they'll grow up, get married, and have sex to bear children, but until then they are kept in the dark and too often admonished for showing an interest. For example, most girls know nothing about the clitoris and are told that masturbation is something only a "slut" or a "whore" would do. Some parents fear that if a girl learns about her clitoris and starts to masturbate, she will become sexually active, get pregnant, have a terrible reputation, and ruin her life. The paradox of this issue is that 60 percent of all males and females in America have intercourse by age sixteen, even though sexual abstinence is still taught in schools and funded by the government.

Sweden begins sex education at the preschool level, continues it through grade twelve, and contraception is provided free by the government.[3] The Netherlands also provides free contraception to teens. Neither the Netherlands nor Sweden teaches sexual abstinence, but they have the lowest teen pregnancy rate among all industrialized nations.[4] In America, boys strive to get "laid" and lose their virginity, while girls are taught to preserve their virginity until marriage. Although boys are not encouraged to have sex before marriage, premarital sex does not carry the same stigma for boys as it does for girls. Boys don't have to worry about their reputations, and sexually active high school boys are often labeled "playboys" or "studs." Not so for girls, whose very reputation could be ruined by having sex and being tagged as a "slut" or a "whore."[5]

Think about the negative scripting to control a girl's sexuality. This "virgin doctrine" for Western civilization is rooted in the Virgin Mary, who is still highly promoted as the ideal for all women. The Eve propaganda also can contribute to a girl's inhibition and fear of her sexuality. Even the celibacy vows for priests and nuns suggest that to abstain from all sexual pleasure is somehow a virtue, even though it is obviously abnormal and unnatural. Boys discover the pleasure of their penis very early and start to masturbate and experience orgasm as soon as they are able. Most girls never masturbate. They do not even know about such a thing. They usually learn about it from a boyfriend. It is not surprising to learn how many women do not have sex because they feel it is "dirty" and wrong. It is even more surprising how many women cannot experience orgasm, or they can but with no consistency.[6]

Women were handed confusing messages about their sexuality from the New Testament, which labeled them as transgressors since they were descendants of Eve, and during the Middle Ages women were regarded as witches and psychics. During the Victorian period women were denied any sexual feelings, and their bodies had to be covered to protect men from temptation as Eve had lured Adam to sin.

THE FEMALE ORGASMIC CONTROVERSY

Historically, there was controversy over female orgasm. Women, even passionate ones, unable to have an orgasm were labeled "frigid." The passionately frigid female was a woman who liked men and loved sex but always stopped short of a climax. As a therapist, I prefer to refer to these women as "pre-orgasmic," meaning a woman who has not had an orgasm but can if willing to learn. Thanks to modern research, these women can now be helped to experience sexual fulfillment.

Let us go back in history to the female orgasmic controversy, which was started by Sigmund Freud. Dr. Freud's theory was that women had two kinds of orgasms, clitoral and vaginal. In his judgment the clitoral orgasm was an immature orgasm that did not require a penis to penetrate, whereas the "mature" vaginal orgasm was stimulated by the male phallus.[7] He taught that women who could not reach orgasm, or could only experience an orgasm through stimulation of the clitoris, possessed some deep-seated unconscious anger and hostility toward their fathers. They could not surrender to the male penis because it represented their father's maleness, and that only a vaginal orgasm was mature and acceptable. Think about what this meant: that women who climaxed without vaginal orgasm stimulated by the male penis were immature and had not resolved their subconscious issues with their fathers. Clitoral orgasms were unacceptable, and women were made to feel guilty about having the wrong kind of orgasm. The cure for this problem of being "frigid" was to submit to psychoanalysis to work through and resolve any subconscious issues with her father.

Another player in the female orgasmic controversy was a woman psychoanalyst by the name of Marie Robinson, who ascribed to Freud's theory about the two orgasms and authored the book *The Power of Sexual Surrender*.[8] What made her book so valuable was her ability to adapt Freud's technical and academic style and then communicate his theory with suitable illustrations so that anyone with a high school education could read and understand the Freudian theory. She used examples from case files of women who grew up with fathers with whom they did not get along, and when they reached adulthood were unable to experience a vaginal orgasm. Like Freud, Robinson believed that the vaginal orgasm was the only legitimate orgasm and that the cure was through psychoanalysis, which could take up to five years of treatment to correct. Dr. Robinson's book became a bestseller, and many women entered treatment to resolve their sexual dysfunction. For Robinson, the woman had to resolve all subconscious resistance to surrendering to the male in order to achieve a vaginal orgasm.[9]

THE IMPORTANT USE OF THE PUBOCOCCYGEUS MUSCLE

Dr. Arnold Kegel, professor emeritus, was a gynecologist from the University of Southern California School of Medicine who was researching and treating women suffering from urinary incontinence. Urinary incontinence is a problem that triggers extreme social embarrassment for the woman because she involuntarily urinates whenever she laughs, coughs, sneezes, or makes any sudden movement.

In female anatomy, there is a band of muscle that connects to the tailbone, or coccyx; called the pubococcygeus muscle, it stretches between a woman's legs and connects to her pubic bone. There are three canal openings in this band of muscle, and a sphincter controls each opening: the urinary sphincter, the vaginal sphincter, and the anal sphincter. Kegel discovered that if the pubococcygeus muscle is weak, it cannot squeeze the urinary sphincter tight enough to keep from urinating whenever it was pressured. The problem was to figure out how to strengthen the pubococcygeus muscle, and no known exercise could do it. Even women who were physically fit and in otherwise good condition could have a weak pubococcygeus muscle. Conversely, women in poor condition and even obese could have a strong pubococcygeus muscle. Kegel developed exercises to strengthen the muscle, which today are known as the "Kegel squeezes." His patients received significantly positive results, and many of the women completely stopped involuntarily urination. Then something surprising and completely unforeseen occurred! Many of the women in this group informed Kegel that they had experienced vaginal orgasm for the very first time; others revealed that they were achieving more orgasms than normal. At first Kegel thought the association of achieving orgasm as a result of the exercises prescribed for incontinence was merely coincidental, but the continuous comments attesting to a relationship between the exercises and sexual climax finally convinced him to investigate further. Kegel selected a group of one thousand women who were diagnosed by clinicians as nonorgasmic, and who by their own testimony had never experienced an orgasm. He taught these women the squeezing exercises and explained the importance of building an orgasmic platform. The orgasmic platform is similar to the excitement stage in Masters and Johnson's four-phase sexual response cycle we discussed in chapter 2—that before orgasm can take place, a woman needs to get into a deep erotic state to create the necessary physiological changes. The orgasmic platform involves those changes, such as swelling of the inner lining of the vaginal walls created by increased blood flow during a deep erotic state. Kegel taught these women to focus on erotic sensations to deepen and intensify their sexual feelings. He educated them about the physiological changes that must take place to reach orgasm, and about the importance of getting in "heat" to enable the blood to flow to the pelvic area. This blood flow permits the labia (lips) majora and minora to engorge with blood and lubricate the flow from the woman's pores, causing the walls of the vaginal canal to fill with blood and become moist and warm. The vaginal sphincter relaxes, and the clitoris becomes erect as it fills with blood. He also taught them to focus on increasing sexual tension. The result—650 of the 1,000 women in the control group achieved their first orgasm, and 65 percent is significant research. [10]

What makes the Kegel squeeze important? Nerve endings related to sexual stimulation are located in the outer third of the vaginal canal, which is the area for sexual stimulation. A woman can feel sexual sensation behind the vaginal sphincter, and pressure behind the ring of the sphincter muscle will give her a pleasurable sensation. If you visualize the vaginal muscle as a clock, the area of sensation is between four and eight o'clock. Some women report sensation at all points of the dial. [11] Kegel believed the pubococcygeus needed to be in good condition so that a woman could squeeze on the penis and receive more sensation during intercourse. He felt that women could not fully experience the sensation if their muscle was not strong or they were not using it during sex. [12]

Most important, the women in this group were not treated with psychotherapy but were instead given a comprehensive sex education that included information about their body and how it functions sexually. Kegel felt strongly that education surpassed the need for therapy. [13] His research questioned the need for psychotherapy for pre-orgasmic women and supported the view that education was what most women needed. [14] The issue was not about their relationship with their fathers, but rather the ignorance that originates from our culture about sex and sexuality—the negative sexual scripting that keeps women from enjoying sex.

Masters and Johnson's research ended the orgasmic controversy by producing hard data on the physiology of intercourse that was revolutionary at the time. Their research ended the orgasmic controversy by finding that women do not have two kinds of orgasms. They have only one kind of orgasm and many erogenous zones that can trigger their orgasm. Masters and Johnson recorded some ten thousand female orgasms and found that pelvic contractions always take place when a woman has an orgasm. [15]

Some women reach orgasm through breast stimulation or through stimulation of the nipples of their breasts. Others are aroused by deep kissing. Many women experience climax from clitoral stimulation or through intercourse, and some have orgasms in their sleep that are triggered by an erotic dream. Whatever the trigger, the orgasm is always the same physiological response: pelvic contractions. With each contraction, there is a surge of pleasurable feeling and a release of sexual tension. There is one orgasm but many different triggers. Masters and Johnson also found that the most intense orgasms originated from masturbation rather than sexual intercourse. The primary "hot button," or erogenous zone, for all women is the clitoris; when stimulated it is where 80 percent of women reach orgasm. Even during intercourse, the movement of fatty tissue surrounding the clitoris can be stimulated by stroking and result in orgasm.

Masters and Johnson taught that women should not surrender to their male partner but to her own lust.[16] When the neurons related to sexual orgasm are stimulated to reach their threshold, they automatically explode into orgasm. A woman does not reach orgasm by thinking about having one but by building enough sexual tension to "fire" the orgasmic neurons. To build sexual tension, she does not focus on her partner but instead on her own erogenous zones that stimulate sexual tension. Whatever she does when having sex, it should be increasing her sexual pleasure and tension. It is equally important that whatever her partner is doing does not distract her from building her own erotic excitement. If he is disturbing her sensate focus, she should tell him. When having sex, there should be nothing going on that is distracting or breaking one's focus on building sexual tension. Anything spoken should be in erotic language to maintain the sexual feeling.

In the discussion on masturbation in chapter 5, we will point out how masturbation is helpful as a training exercise in learning how to be erotically focused. The ability to masturbate teaches you how to focus on and surrender to lust. When engaged in sexual intercourse, you transfer into your relationship what you do during self-sex. Masturbation is a form of self-foreplay, and during sex with your partner you need just as much or more foreplay to get into erotic reality at a level that prepares you for orgasm when intercourse begins. Foreplay is one of the most important activities that couples should prolong prior to the actual act of intercourse.

THE G-SPOT

Lastly, we need to recognize Whipple and Perry as the two people who brought the controversial "G-spot" to popular attention. They did not discover the G-spot; they were the researchers who brought it to everyone's attention. Gynecologist Ernst Gräfenberg discovered the G-spot in the 1950s, but after his death it was Whipple and Perry who named the spot for him and published a book that created a lot of controversy.[17] Today there is some debate about whether the G-spot is real. The consensus is that some women do have a G-spot, while it is dormant and still undiscovered in others.

So, what is the G-spot? It is another erogenous zone along the anterior wall of the vagina, located about an inch or so into the front wall of the outer third of the vagina. Stimulation of this area can trigger orgasm, which often accompanies an ejaculation of a clear fluid.[18] This fluid neither looks nor smells like urine, nor does it stain sheets like urine. You can purchase a G-spot finder through sex accessory stores. This little tool helps you reach and stimulate the G-spot area; the tool may even awaken a dormant G-spot.

Masters and Johnson felt that if a woman could reach orgasm in masturbation but not during intercourse, she was dysfunctional. If she could reach orgasm during intercourse but not when masturbating, she was equally dysfunctional. A woman who could not reach orgasm at all was also considered sexually dysfunctional. In other words, a fully sexually functioning woman, who is liberated from all negative sexual scripting, enjoys sex and can reach orgasm with or without a partner.[19]

GETTING INTO EROTICA TO BECOME EROTIC

For a woman to be able to fulfill herself sexually, she must learn to enjoy the pleasure centers of her body by freeing herself from all inhibition, fear, and embarrassment. To successfully accomplish this, she needs to read and view erotic material: books, magazines, and films. Sex should be the focus of her mind, and she must arrive at a place where she gives herself permission to indulge in sexual pleasure either by herself or with a partner. She needs to learn how to surrender to her lust, to her desire, and to her sexual sensations when having sex. Instead of focusing entirely on her partner, she should be aware of the erotic sensations *she* is feeling. By surrendering to her libido, she is aware of being an erotically sexual person who is both competent and capable of giving and receiving sexual pleasure. She must also give herself permission to have sexual thoughts and fantasies. Erotic films and reading material can be a real turn-on. She must also get comfortable with the use of erotic language, as it is much more difficult to reach orgasm when your mind is heavily guarded against anything sexual. For that matter, it is difficult to even desire sex when you keep your heart "clean" and your mind "pure," which is why "good girls" have a harder time enjoying sex than "bad girls." A major struggle for women today is the overwhelming sense of responsibility for family and a career. The difficulty in balancing these responsibilities while trying to relax and make time for yourself prevents you from focusing on erotic pleasure.

Women have been more influenced by the Adam and Eve mythology of the Bible than they realize. The Eve scripting has been present in Western culture since the first century. Saint Paul talked about Eve being the "transgressor," and Saint Augustine and Saint Thomas Aquinas expanded on that idea in their teachings. It is this very fear of being like Eve that helps fuel the double standard in our culture between men and women. A male who enjoys his sexuality is not seen as a slut or a whore, but a female who enjoys her sexuality risks having derogatory labels attached to her reputation.[20] All too often I've had a couple seated in my office when the husband looks at his new bride and asks her to tell him how many men she had sex with before they started dating. When the wife is truthful and tells him he's acting like a wounded puppy, he starts to feel threatened and upset that she was a "whore."

Think how different it would be for women if a different interpretation of Eve were to be presented. Eve, in my opinion, was adventurous and intelligent. She found the Garden of Eden boring but beautiful and had learned that being good all the time was equally unexciting. She needed more.

Eve was a woman with ambition and insight, and she was aware of her sexuality. She thought if the Lord designed the clitoris, then He must have meant for her to use it. Surely if the Lord created sexuality, He created it for a purpose. Finally, Eve took a risk that gave her and Adam a renewed sense of life and adventure and excitement. Most of all, she gave Adam more pleasure than he had ever received in that damn Garden! Although they were forced out of the Garden of Eden, they took pleasure in their sexuality and great enjoyment in having children. When they left the Garden, they never looked back. Adam and Eve never missed the Garden of Eden because they had each other and their children. Had it not been for Eve's risk taking, they never would have progressed past the monotony of the Garden.

Eve should be every woman's heroine! She was the first feminist, who sexually liberated herself and Adam. Although she was condemned for her actions, it was the negative sexual script that was responsible for her condemnation—the "erotophobes." The lesson from Eve: If women want to be sexually liberated, they need to get out of the "Garden of Conventional Thinking" and break their commitment to propriety.

It takes a lot of work and experience for women to become sexually self-actualized, and it's especially difficult to permit themselves to be "deviant" from the teachings of the negative script.

5

SOLO SEX

Becoming Erotic with Yourself

HOW MASTURBATION TEACHES US HOW TO MAKE ORGASMS

Pauline looks at me with a smile, and then with a confident but almost prideful tone she tells me, "I started masturbating when I was around five or six years old. I've been having orgasms ever since I can remember." She was having orgasms before she even knew what sex was all about. She discovered this pleasure center on her body, and rubbing it felt good.

As a teenager, Pauline had sex with her boyfriend, and if she didn't come she would unabashedly masturbate in front of him until she was satisfied. In her late teens she was having multiple orgasms fairly consistently. Pauline learned to appreciate and enjoy her body. She felt comfortable in the nude and felt no shame about her looks. All the practice she had in solo sex gave her the knowledge and confidence to satisfy herself in social sex.

Sex for Pauline was pleasurable and relaxing. It provided a wonderful escape from stress and a profound release of tension. After sex she felt calm and at peace, and her sexuality was integrated into her life. It was as much a priority as eating, drinking, and exercising. Her husband confirmed that with Pauline, he experienced the best sex he had ever known. He had listened to her and was open to learning how to turn her on and help her reach satisfaction. She had no inhibitions about satisfying him, and there was nothing she would not do with him sexually.

Pauline found and embraced her sexuality without the aid of books, teachers, parents, or a boyfriend. She learned through self-discovery and had the fortitude to experiment and not let the negative voices prevent her from following her instincts and her natural curiosity. Although she didn't mention it, I am sure she found bits and pieces of information here and there to support what she was discovering on her own. With all the negative messages from our culture about sex being sinful or naughty, and even with the threatening peril of becoming a slut or a whore, she pursued her interest in her body with an acceptance that most young girls would feel too guilty and fearful to do. She also ignored the negative sexual script of America, even challenged it. Like Eve in the Garden, she fearlessly ate the apple! From Pauline's experience, we understand the importance of a woman's need to bite the apple and disregard the garden of conventional propaganda.

Why should sex be considered "social"? When we think of sex, we usually think of sex with another person. But there are two kinds of sex: solo sex and social sex. Social sex involves a partner, whereas solo sex is self-satisfaction, or "masturbation." The fact is, we can enjoy the benefits of both, since one form is not better than another. Both forms are meaningful and pleasurable, but a different experience. Having sex with a partner provides the added physical stimulation of the other person as we experience the connection to our partner's life spirit. It is stimulating to not only be touched by someone else but also to experience their own erotic responses. We're all connected to our inner self, both psychologically and physically. The psychological connection involves thinking and self-talk, and we are physically connected when we feel physical pain or pleasure. We also have a sexual relationship with ourselves when we feel aroused and have the desire to mate. We experience sexual tension and feel "sexy" or "horny." We have personal fantasies, dreams, wishes, fears, and feelings. Sex with our self is a private meeting with our inner being, a very personal experience that is also spiritual. Only self-sex offers the connection between body and spirit.

In solo sex (or self-sex) you have no distraction because you are not negotiating with a partner and can fully focus and concentrate on your desire. Many people, women especially, have no conception of the benefits of solo sex. Sexual science now recognizes that self-sex is not harmful and can even be beneficial to your physical and psychological health.

Science has discovered that sexual orgasms have healing power in addition to offering pleasure. Sex can improve the immune system by releasing antioxidants; it also relieves pain. Orgasms release endorphins, a natural painkiller, and can alleviate headaches and tension. Even getting yourself into a deep erotic state can improve your threshold for pain. Orgasm helps reduce pelvic congestion and vasocongestion, which causes menstrual cramps.

There are many more reasons for encouraging solo sex as an ongoing life experience. There are no interpersonal risks, no hurt feeling, and no rejection or guilt for failing to please your partner. It is not always practical or convenient to have sexual intercourse; your partner may be ill or feel tired or just not in the mood. He may also be out of town and unavailable, or you may be traveling solo. Solo sex is so practical and convenient. With solo sex, you negotiate just with yourself!

Masters and Johnson's research found that the strongest, most intense orgasms are experienced during self-sex because it eliminates the distractions of a partner, we can stay more focused on what arouses us, and we can stimulate ourselves to peak excitement.

People of all ages should take pleasure in life. We all experience stress and pain and suffering, and pleasure is an important counterbalance to stress and suffering. Adults and children alike can endure unimaginable amounts of stress and pain; pleasure is one of the sources of light that releases you from the darkness in life.

In chapter 1 we talked about how the Egyptians celebrated masturbation by honoring their creator god, Atum. They believed that the creation of the universe began from his ejaculate. Masturbation was not a negative issue for the Egyptians, but the official position of the Catholic Church on masturbation is that it's a mortal sin. Whereas venial sins, like misdemeanors, are pardonable by the Church, mortal sins are like felonies and bring on a sentence of death. In 1976 the Vatican declared that masturbation is an "intrinsically and seriously disordered act," and in 1993 Pope John Paul II condemned masturbation as morally wrong. Likewise, most fundamentalist Protestant Christians condemn masturbation as sinful and morally wrong.[1] In matters of sexuality, the Christian Church has traditionally had great difficulty. While churches make a significant contribution to charity and the welfare of others, church doctrine appears obsessed with sexual issues, making it difficult not to be critical of their negative script. Moreover, people other than Christians also feel negatively about masturbation. Where did these negative feelings originate? Certainly not from the Egyptians! The negativity about masturbation is another symptom created by the advocates of the negative sexual script. You may remember that in 1994, President Bill Clinton fired Surgeon General Jocelyn Elder when she said on television that masturbation should be taught as part of human sexuality?[2] Why was her public statement bad? Who did it offend and why? Who are the people behind the outrage to silence her? They are authorities and institutions from the Middle Ages to this twenty-first century, all of whom helped to further fear, guilt, shame, inhibition, and ignorance about anything sexual. These are the writers and advocates of the negative sexual script.

ONAN AND GENESIS 38:7–10

There is no teaching in the Bible about masturbation, but there is one passage in the Old Testament that is continually corrupted by clergymen, priests, and laymen. The passage is found in Genesis 38:7–10. In this story God kills Er, the firstborn son of Judah. "And then Judah said to Onan, 'Sleep with your brother's wife and fulfill your duty to her as a brother-in-law to raise up offspring for your brother.' But Onan knew the child would not be his, so whenever he slept with his brother's wife, he spilled his semen on the ground to keep from providing offspring for his brother. But what he did was wicked too, and so the Lord put him to death also."

Some people have taken this passage to mean that masturbation is wrong. Others have interpreted the passage as condemning coitus interruptus, the withdrawal method of birth control, which is what Onan actually did. In this passage, Jewish scholars interpret the condemnation of Onan as Onan's disobedience and deception in not following the Jewish tradition of fathering his brother's child.[3]

It is important to remember that the Old Testament is a Jewish book, not a Christian book, and was written by Jews centuries before Christianity came into existence. For that reason, we should accept Jewish scholarship on this matter. To interpret this passage as God's condemnation of masturbation, or the use of birth control, is again taking a verse out of context and exploiting it for one's own biased view.

Dutch theologian Dr. Balthazar Bekker coined the term "onanism" as a synonym for "masturbation." He wrote a pamphlet in 1710 entitled *Onania, the Heinous Sin of Self-Pollution and All Its Frightful Consequences for Both Sexes, Considered with Spiritual and Physical Advice*.[4] Other pamphlets followed, which were written by noted physicians and the best authorities of their time.

Samuel David Tissot, a European medical doctor and a devout Catholic, believed that masturbation was not only morally wrong as the Church taught but that it also was "self-abuse" and seriously injurious to a person's physical health because of the habitual loss of semen.[5]

WHEN SEX WAS WRONGLY BELIEVED TO BE UNHEALTHY

Benjamin Rush, the founder of American Psychiatry and President George Washington's personal physician, published an article that illustrated how masturbation caused mental illness, epilepsy, impotence, and even death.[6] Other physicians followed what ultimately became a false belief that many illnesses, diseases, and unexplained symptoms were the result of masturbation. When medicine joined religion in condemning masturbation, medical doctors, priests, and ministers condemned the practice as destructive to your health and soul. B. G. Jefferis, MD, PhD, published a book titled *Safe Counsel*, which had thirty-nine editions between 1893 and 1928. The book was very critical of masturbation as a health hazard.[7]

Jefferis provided what now is known to be false and incorrect information, but his book and others were read by millions of people. Jefferis taught that the fluid of the testes contained important nutrition, and that the male body must maintain and protect what we refer to today as the immune system. The belief was that whenever a male ejaculated, he discharged the "healthy" fluids produced by the testes and which were needed to maintain a healthy body. It was thought that the loss of semen would make men vulnerable to disease and physical weakness, and that they could even go blind, lose all physical strength, suffer dementia, or develop epilepsy or tuberculosis.

For women, masturbation would cause brain damage, which in turn could cause blindness or dementia. It could subject women to attacks of hysteria, stomach pain, ulceration of the uterus, or elongation of the clitoris, which, Tissot believed, would also deprive them of modesty and reason.[8]

J. F. Kellogg, a medical doctor who played an important role in the anti-masturbation crusade, traveled the country while lecturing about the serious health dangers for people who committed such evil acts. He invented what came to be marketed as Corn Flakes in the hope that the cereal would help restore the nutrition lost from discharge when masturbating. He also believed that the cereal was bland enough to curb sexual desire and thus lessen the urge to masturbate.[9] Another belief during the anti-masturbation crusade was that spicy foods and red meat stimulated sexual desire, so it was recommended that people eat only very bland food. The Rev. Sylvester Graham encouraged the use of whole-wheat flour to replace lost nutrition from masturbation, and his name is still on the "graham cracker."[10]

Frightened parents bought devices designed to keep children from touching their genitals, such as wire cages that locked around a child like jockey shorts so that a child could not easily touch himself or herself. There were about twenty or more contraptions invented to prevent masturbation and many treatment methods thought to cure masturbation—everything from cages to electrical shock to putting pure carbolic acid on the clitoris to tying a child's hands. Using pins to close the foreskin, sewing the foreskin shut to prevent erections, and injections of silver nitrate into the urethra for cauterization—all were recommended methods to prevent masturbation.[11]

This crusade went even beyond masturbation. Married couples were told not to have sex more than a dozen times a year, as it was believed that sexual excess was harmful. It was also believed that "violent" contractions from orgasm damaged the brain, the cardiovascular system, and the nervous system. Most of society was deluded by the most respected and trusted social leaders, many of whom were clergymen, teachers, and doctors. Some authorities did not join the crusade and were not on the anti-masturbation bandwagon. Two of the most recognized were Havelock Ellis, MD, and Dr. Sigmund Freud.[12] The anti-masturbation leaders of this movement were deluded but convinced, and they deceived the public. Although these teachings and beliefs were fallacious, Americans became fearful about self-abuse, and those who dared to masturbate were believed to be mentally ill—immoral, sick, and disturbed. Anything sexual became stigmatized and too embarrassing to mention, whether talking about sex or even reading about the subject. All information on sexuality was censored and hidden, since it was feared that having sexual information or even just talking about sex might be sexually stimulating and ultimately harmful.

Even when medical science realized and reported that these beliefs were false, society continued to ignore those findings. The response to the publication of Alfred Kinsey's survey on male sexuality in 1948 was overwhelmingly negative[13] because many Americans considered it profoundly disturbing. One of the surprising findings was the sheer numbers of Americans who admitted to masturbating; even more enlightening was the fact that these "masturbators" were neither becoming ill nor dropping dead! Nothing abnormal was happening to these otherwise "responsible" citizens. They worked and contributed to the good of society and had none of the symptoms attributed to masturbation. Medical science had found answers for the symptoms that had been wrongly ascribed to onanism. Once medical science had discovered germs and bacteria, practitioners no longer felt that masturbation was harmful to a person's health and general well-being. Moreover, science gained the capability to study semen and discovered that the ejaculate was simply a fluid to help transport sperm.

REASONS FOR MASTURBATING

We now know that masturbation is not harmful; in fact, it is beneficial to our physical and psychological health. Since everyone would benefit from masturbation throughout his or her life span, I have compiled twenty reasons masturbation is so beneficial to individuals, couples, and society.

Twenty Reasons Masturbation Is Healthy and Beneficial

1. **Masturbation Is Pleasurable.** It is most important that people of every age experience pleasure. When you're enjoying yourself, you feel good about living and are enjoying life. We all have

stress, pain, and suffering in our lives, and pleasure is an important counterbalance to the stress and struggle of living. Adults and children alike can successfully endure incredible stress and suffering if it is counterbalanced with pleasure, joy, and meaning, and sexual orgasm is the ultimate pleasure experience. If you can have orgasmic experiences with yourself, you'll enjoy nonsexual experiences even more. It is the ultimate pleasure that gives you permission to experience other nonsexual pleasures. Pleasure is the light that releases you from the darkness in life.

2. **Masturbation Releases Sexual Tension.** As sexual beings we were designed like all other living things to procreate, and each of us has a biological urge to mate. We are biologically hardwired to be sexually aroused and "turned on" to desiring sex. It is normal and natural to experience lust, which creates sexual tension that can prevent us from being able to sleep, concentrate, focus on something important, or just plain relax. Masturbation is an easy release to sexual tension.

3. **Masturbation Releases Stressful Tension.** Masturbation can act as a relaxation technique. Everyday reality can be stressful, causing a buildup of anxieties and worries. Tensions related to things you must do or things you feel went wrong with your day can leave you in a stressful state. You can be bothered with relationship issues and family affairs. When you move from these daily realities to erotic reality, something changes. All the daily reality issues fade into the background and erotic thoughts and fantasies come into the foreground. Erotic thoughts and feelings trump the stressors of everyday life. They put you in a different mental and emotional state. Many people find masturbating just before going to sleep helps provide the relaxation needed to fall asleep.

4. **Masturbation Improves Sexual Capability and Competency.** I believe that masturbation is the first step toward sexual competency. Through self-sex you can learn how to respond to sexual stimuli, which helps you learn how to put yourself into a deep state of erotic arousal. It is one of the most helpful ways to work out inhibitions, guilt, and fears about surrendering totally to your sexual desire. Just as you can learn how to have an orgasm, you also can learn how to climax more frequently and efficiently.

Masturbation is a wonderful "hands on" (pun intended) way to practice shifting from daily reality to erotic reality. It also is the best preparation for engaging in sex with a partner, since much of what you do in masturbation can be transferred to a sexual relationship. Imagine a woman who kept her vow of abstinence until marriage. She has never masturbated and has never had an orgasm. Then imagine a woman who has kept her vow to be abstinent until marriage but masturbated regularly to orgasm during her single years. Which of these two women would be most competent on her wedding night? Which would be the most relaxed and responsive to her husband's touching? Which one is most likely to experience an orgasm on her wedding night?

5. **Masturbation Maintains Your Sexual Functioning and Sexual Fitness.** Masturbation keeps you tuned up sexually. It keeps you mindful of your sexuality so that it does not become lost in everyday reality. Masters and Johnson have said that our sexual system needs to be exercised and used regularly if it is to keep functioning and not dry up, especially as we age. As we grow older, our libido starts to diminish. Masters and Johnson used the phrase "Use it or lose it" when it comes to sexual ability and growing old.[14]

6. **Masturbation Helps Maintain a Healthy Prostate Gland.** Whenever a male ejaculates, he flushes out impurities in the pores of the prostate gland, which also makes for a healthier prostate.[15]

7. **Masturbation Provides an Alternative Form of Sexual Experience.** There are two kinds of sexual experiences, solo sex and social sex; both are enjoyable but different. The two forms of sexual experience are equally unique and pleasurable, and there are advantages and disadvantages to both. For example, with solo sex you don't have to negotiate with a partner but can fully focus and concentrate on your desire. In social sex you have the pleasure of experiencing your partner's responses, which can enhance the reality of the event.

8. **Masturbation Provides a Private and Personal Meaning with Yourself.** We each have a relationship with ourselves. We have personal fantasies, dreams, wishes, fears, feelings, and joys. We all have a sense of life spirit, a life energy that is our inner

self. We have a sexual relationship with ourself, and often our first erotic experience is imprinted in our psyche. We are able to recall all our erotic experiences and even fantasies of new experiences. Self-sex is a private meeting with our inner being, a very personal pleasure that is akin to a mystical or spiritual experience. No other experience in life offers you the sense of connection between your body and your spirit as an orgasm. The mind and body are one, which is both private and personal. Masturbation requires an intercommunication.

9. **Masturbation Is Practical and Convenient.** It is not always practical, convenient, or even possible to have social sex. You may not have a suitable partner, or your partner may be sick or too tired. He or she also may be busy working, away on business, or not in the mood. You also may be on a trip and without a partner. Masturbation is practical and convenient, and the only person you have to negotiate with for sex is you! If you are single, unmarried, and/or not in a relationship, you can still have a meaningful sex life—with yourself.

10. **Masturbation Provides an Alternative Form of Sexual Variety with Your Partner.** Masturbating with your partner or mutually masturbating each other can be a very intimate sexual experience. There is something shared in that experience that is even more personal than what is shared during sexual intercourse. You are allowing your partner to see your most private sex life, the sex life you usually keep hidden and out of view. In addition, during times when you cannot have intercourse with your partner (i.e., immediately after your partner has given birth to a baby or when treating a vaginal yeast infection) mutual masturbation can provide a very pleasurable sexual experience. In addition, if the male should reach orgasm first, he can masturbate his female partner to satisfaction. In cases where the male cannot get an erection, he can still satisfy his female partner.

11. **Masturbation Eliminates the Fear and Risk of Pregnancy.** Masturbation can be a source for sexual pleasure and release when a couple has no safe means of birth control.

12. **Masturbation Saves the Cost of Birth Control.** Birth control is expensive, especially for teenagers and young people.

13. **Masturbation Can Be Helpful in "Saving" a Person's Virginity.** For couples that want to wait until marriage before they have intercourse, mutual masturbation can help them release sexual tension without violating their vow to maintain virginity until marriage.

14. **Masturbation Eliminates the Risk of Getting a Sexually Transmitted Disease.** If you do not know your partner's sexual history and want to protect yourself from getting a sexually transmitted disease, masturbation could be a way to release sexual tension without risking disease.

15. **Masturbation Has No Interpersonal Risks.** There are no interpersonal risks in having self-sex, and no hurt feelings of rejection or guilt from failure to please your partner. In masturbation, you have none of the interpersonal politics that can make a sexual experience negative and unrewarding.

16. **Masturbation Provides a Sexual Experience with No Performance Anxiety.** There is no performance pressure in masturbation as one can feel in social sex. There is no need to fake an orgasm, nor any need to worry about whether you look presentable. There is no problem or fear of sexual dysfunction, like getting it up, keeping it up, or being able to release at the appropriate time.

17. **Masturbation Provides the Most Intense Orgasms.** Masters and Johnson's studies found that in masturbation, we have the strongest orgasms because there are no distractions of a partner, and we can stay focused directly on what arouses us. We also can stimulate ourselves to peak excitement without having to negotiate with a partner.

18. **Masturbation Helps Prevent Sex Crimes.** When Denmark legalized pornography, there was a 68 percent drop in sex crimes. When Japan did the same, rapes fell from 4,677 per year to 1,500 per year. In America, the states with the greatest access to pornography have shown a 53 percent drop in sex crimes. Conversely, states with the least access to pornography have seen a rise in sex crimes by 27 percent. Because masturbation is an outlet for sexual tension, it helps prevent sex crime.[16]

19. **Masturbation Can Help Relieve Cramps during Menstruation.** Orgasm helps reduce pelvic congestion and vasocongestion

that cause menstrual cramps. When a woman is having menstrual cramps, masturbating to orgasm will often relieve them.

20. **Masturbation Is Important to Maintaining Good Health.** Sex scientists have discovered that sexual orgasms have healing power. Sex can improve the immune system by releasing antioxidants. Sex can also relieve pain, since orgasms release endorphins, a natural painkiller. Orgasm can stop headaches, relieve tension, and make us feel better psychologically.

Studies done by Beverly Whipple, PhD, an associate professor at Rutgers University, found that "orgasm is a natural analgesic." Her research with women suffering from chronic arthritis and other painful conditions found that masturbating to orgasm or achieving orgasm through intercourse and just getting in a deep erotic state improved their threshold for pain.[17] We have come to the realization that masturbation is not just harmless but also beneficial to our health.[18] It is especially beneficial to our sexual health. Masturbation should be taught as a part of our sexuality. It should also be taught as something that is very important to our physical health and our psychological well-being.

Masturbation should be our first sexual experience and the beginning of our sexual journey. After we have learned how to put ourself into a deep erotic state and have orgasms, we are then ready for social sex. While we may not be emotionally and psychologically ready for sex with someone else, we can rehearse and prepare for social sex by engaging in solo sex. When we finally meet the right partner and feel ready for sex, we can transfer much of what we have learned in masturbation to our relational experience. That is another reason masturbation should be taught as something beneficial.

6

UNDERSTANDING MALE SEXUALITY

David and Lisa have been married for five years. Lisa does not like pornography and has never masturbated. She cannot feel like having sex unless she feels closely connected to David. She only likes the traditional sexual position of the man on top. Rear entry is out of the question. Her belief is that the "doggie" position is for dogs, not humans. She does not like oral sex. She believes the penis was designed to be put in a vagina and no place else. She does not like it when David tries to stimulate her orally. She thinks she has experienced orgasm but is not certain.

David has had five years of sexual frustration. He feels sexual tension every day. Most of the time, his sexual advances toward Lisa are rejected. Although he believes it is wrong, he finds himself masturbating several times a week. The truth is, he has more sex with himself than he does with his wife. He senses Lisa's discomfort and inhibitions. He has had to inhibit his responses and hold back experimenting with things he feels are sexually exciting. He hides his practice of looking at pornography because he knows that Lisa would never approve.

Although he is sexually frustrated, he still loves Lisa and wants to have children with her and start a family. Paradoxically, he continually thinks of having sex with other women. In his sexual fantasies, the fantasy woman desires sex as much as or even more than he does. It is as though David has two lives. One life is the real life he has with Lisa, which is stable and grounded in family values. Lisa is instrumental in helping him create a home. Her income from her work, combined with his, enables them to have dinners out, a comfortable life, a nice house and yard, and cars. Together they have made a nest. They enjoy friends. They enjoy each other's families. They plan holidays together. They give each other mutual support and help with all the maintenance that living requires. They help each other with the doubts, fears, and issues that come up from time to time. If you asked David if he loves Lisa, his answer would be a definite "Yes!"

David's other life is mostly fantasy. He has erotic tension every day. There is hardly a day he does not desire to have sex with a woman. He would like it to be with Lisa, but most of the time, Lisa does not seem to be feeling sexual. David sees real live women every day on the street and at his office. For him, sex is everywhere. He has some male friends and some colleagues at work who are often telling sexual jokes or stories about getting laid. They often talk about who they would like to "fuck" if they could. This other world of David's is an erotic world. It is mostly fantasy, but it is still real because he feels sexual frustration every day. He usually gets release from this sexual tension by masturbating in private. David finds pornography helpful in bringing him to a stronger orgasm. Although he wants to have sex with Lisa, her chronic rejections to his advances have made him turn more to having sex with himself. David finds that pornography is a helpful fantasy partner. Enriching his sexual relationship with himself enables him to better accept the sexual frustration he feels with Lisa. He finds himself less angry and resentful. He compensates for their sexual differences with porn and masturbation. This seems to keep him from sexually acting out and having an affair.

Lisa often goes to bed before David. She gets tired, and David stays up to watch one of the late shows on television. Often though, when Lisa goes to bed, David watches pornography on his computer and has sex with himself. He then feels relaxed and can fall asleep almost immediately. One night, Lisa gets up for a drink of water and catches David watching pornography on his computer. She is shocked. She feels angry; she feels hurt; she feels offended; she feels complete disapproval. She feels a rush of confusion and sorrow. She has always thought so highly of David. She had no idea he could do something like watch pornography. For Lisa, it is as though she had caught David with another woman. She reacts as though she had just found out he had been having affairs behind her back. She asks him how long he has been watching porn and if he has ever had a real affair. With tears and resentment, she tells David how she could never compete with one of "those women" in the porn video and asks how could he look at women as sexual objects? David feels so much shame, embarrassment, and guilt that he confesses that he watches porn and masturbates four or five times a week and occasionally more. Lisa feels he is sexually addicted and insists that he go for sexual addiction treatment. Finally, after a long discussion, they agree to first go to a marriage counselor.

The story of David and Lisa is not unique. Many of the clients who come into marriage counseling tell a similar story. The wife or girlfriend finds out that her husband or boyfriend is into pornography. She is usually very upset and threatened by the discovery that "her man" needs to look at sex. What often makes the female more perplexed is the recognition that although she feels they have a great sex life together, he still looks at other women and enjoys looking at pictures or videos of women having sex. Most women have a very difficult time understanding why pornography is so important to men.

THE COMPLEXITY OF MALE SEXUALITY

Male sexuality is very complex. Not only do most women not understand it, but most men do not either. In the twenty-five years I have been teaching human sexuality, I have greatly increased my own understanding. Teaching the subject helped me better understand my own sexuality. Regarding heterosexual male sexuality, there is one axiom that I have found to be almost universally agreed upon. In discussions with heterosexual men, it seems an accepted general truth that most men feel sexual frustration almost every day. Males have what appears to be a hypersensitivity to sexuality. Males are biologically hardwired to plant their seed everywhere they can. Nature or, if you prefer, God, wanted to guarantee procreation. All nature cares about is procreation. The male brain is hardwired to make sure that seed will be planted and life will continue. Men are not naturally monogamous. They were designed by nature to plant their seed everywhere they can. They are the sowers of seed. They are wired to be procreators.

Heterosexual males can be sexually stimulated by almost anything that looks or resembles a female. Even color, smell, and sound can sexually excite a man. Sigmund Freud believed that we are all "polymorphous perverse." He believed that many forms of stimulation could sexually arouse people.[1] I have come to believe that men are more hormonal than women. The hormone is testosterone. When men get "horny" or "turned on," they become "in heat." Sexual desire and frustration becomes an "itch" they want to scratch. Their foreground is heavily influenced by erotic feelings and desire for sex. When a man feels sexual frustration, his thinking is impaired. Under the influence of his hormones, he will do and say things or behave differently than when he is not "in heat." Men who sexually harass women are not doing it for a feeling of power. That is a very popular but inaccurate notion. With celebrity males, their power is in their potential to ruin a woman's career or make sure she loses her job if she reports the sexual harassment; but they are not sexually harassing women for power, they are sexually harassing them for sex. They employ beautiful women they feel an attraction to and then get "turned on" working close to them. When they become "in heat," their judgment becomes impaired; they start to see their employee as a sex object, and the harassment follows. Often their perception is so distorted by their desire that they think the woman they are harassing likes it and wants it. In their distorted minds, they often think the sexual interaction is consensual.

THE MALE FRUSTRATION AXIOM

The axiom is this: Most males will live with sexual frustration from the time they become sexual until they die. Sexuality has been socialized, and men cannot plant their seed everywhere. In fact, every culture has laws governing sexual practices. There are also social mores that must be respected and followed or there will be both personal and social consequences. Men must learn how to manage their sexual frustration. If they do not, they break laws, which can put them in prison; or they violate mores, which will get them divorced. Violation of the social norms can create chaos, disorder, and discord at a level that can ruin a very good relationship. It has the potential to destroy everything that is good and wonderful in a person's life. Men must learn how to manage their sexual desire and their sexual frustration. Men who don't are the ones who expose their genitals in public, sexually harass women, and even rape; but it's not for power, it's for sex. Certainly, some men who sexually harass women are either narcissistic or become narcissistic when they are "in heat." There is also some question regarding their weakness to maintain the boundaries between what is right and what is wrong.

Most men manage their sexual frustration with pornography and masturbation. Here is another axiom: The use of pornography is a normal part of male sexuality. Heterosexual male sexuality is all about feeling attraction to women. It is also about being sexually stimulated by women. That includes real women as well as pictures, fantasies, and images of women. Most men are easily sexually excited and are responsive to anything sexual. They continually must deal with sexual frustration throughout their lifetime. I have seen men in my clinical practice who were in their eighties and could not achieve an erection, but they still felt sexual tension and the desire to have sex. I have known men who had their prostate gland removed because of cancer. They too could no longer have erections, yet they still felt sexual tension and the desire to have sexual intercourse. The socialization of the sex drive and the laws of culture do not allow full sexual expression. Men must sublimate and masturbate. This is true even when a man is in a very compatible relationship with a woman he loves and with whom he has a satisfying sexual relationship. This may sound like a contradiction, but remember that men never get enough sex. Most women cannot meet a man's sexual needs. Certainly there are exceptions, but I am speaking in general terms. I am referring to averages. I am saying that the majority of married women cannot meet their husband's sexual needs. It is not so much the quality of the sex as much as it is the quantity. Men just do not get enough. While a man may love his wife and love having sex with her, he is not by nature monogamous. As the comedian Chris Rock once said in one of his stand-up routines, "A man's fidelity is as good as his options."[2] When a guy is walking around feeling sexual desire and frustration, it is not easy to turn down an opportunity to get relief. It is not that he does not love his wife; it is just that he is biologically designed to plant his seed whenever the opportunity presents itself. Women must deal with their period each month, but men have to deal with sexual desire and frustration almost daily.

DAVID AND LISA

Let us get back to David and Lisa. There is in Lisa something that is in all women, and there is something in all women that is in Lisa. It is not just the body that attracts men; it is also the femaleness. If David could not be attracted to other women, he could not be attracted to Lisa, because she is a woman. If he can be attracted to Lisa, then he can be attracted to other women.

Heterosexual men are attracted to many women. Men are biologically designed that way. To be attracted to women and to feel desire to plant their seed is the biological essence of male sexuality. It is the natural purpose of libido. This is primary biology in males—the desire to procreate. Men are designed to become easily aroused. What so many women do not realize is that it is not normal for men to think only of one woman. Men's brains are filled with many female images, even former girlfriends, female fantasies, and sex partners. If the understanding in a marriage is that they are to be sexually exclusive with their partner and maintain a commitment to monogamy, men must improve their sexual communication, sexual frequency, and emotional connection to keep their commitment. If a couple defines commitment to include the male not having thoughts and fantasies of other women, that would create extraordinary hypocrisy from the male, because that is impossible for sexually normal males.

PORNOGRAPHY

There are prehistoric sexual drawings on the walls of caves. The Kama Sutra contains beautiful mosaics that date back to 400 CE and explicitly show every conceivable position for having sexual intercourse. Japanese Schunga woodcuts, sculptures, and paintings depict sexual intercourse. The Greeks had an appreciation of the nude body of both men and women. Many of their sports events were performed in the nude, and much of their sculpture and art included nudity. Have you been to Florence, Italy, and seen Michelangelo's *David*? There is nothing left to the imagination with that piece of artwork. Did you know that the Romans wore penis amulets? Not just Roman adults, but also children. The image of a penis was a good-luck charm they believed would protect anyone who wore it. When the Church took control of the Roman Empire, the Saint Christopher medal, still worn by many Catholics today, replaced the penis amulet as a protector and good-luck charm.

America's Puritan and Victorian history labels almost anything sexual as pornographic. That includes even classic art and books with sexual content. America's negative sexual script teaches that we should not view anything that is naked or erotic or sexually arousing. We are not to see sex or fantasize about sex. In fact, it is considered wrong to watch two dogs do it! America has a long history of censorship regarding anything sexual—books, pictures, movies, art, magazines, anything judged to be arousing. Pornography is hard to define because it has a long history in America of being considered sinful and morally wrong. There are exceptions, but most Americans condemn porn and have considerable difficulty with it. Many Americans judge any nudity or display of private parts as porn. If it might be arousing, it's porn!

David and Lisa are a typical example. David and Lisa are still following the negative sexual script, or perhaps it would be more accurate to say that the negative sexual script of our culture is still controlling them.

It is estimated that approximately fifty million or more Americans are viewing pornography on their computers each month. About ten million of those fifty million are women. This does not include those who are viewing porn in books and magazines. It also does not include those who view porn on cable and satellite television. We know that porn magazine sales total more than fifty million dollars a month.

Males watch the majority of porn. It is estimated that 72 percent of males and 28 percent of females visit porn websites monthly. Women's pornography often consists of romance novels containing explicit and graphic sexual descriptions, which some women find very stimulating and arousing. There is also pornography that is made by women for women.

There is nothing that can bring to the forefront all the moral teachings of the negative sexual script than a discussion of pornography or, even more, viewing it! That may explain why it is so controvertible. While millions find it enjoyable, many more millions of Americas condemn it. We have been so brainwashed with negative sexual scripting that most adults cannot show any objectivity about this subject.

In 1965 Supreme Court Justice Potter Stewart stated regarding pornography, "It is difficult to define intelligently, but I know it when I see it!" This kind of subjectivity has inspired the banning of such books as *The Color Purple*, *Our Bodies Ourselves*, and countless others, as well as *Ms.* magazine, from high school libraries.

Americans are not to view anything that is naked or erotic. We are not to read or see anything that may be sexually arousing. We are to have no outlets for sexual expression except for sex with our married partner. That kind of teaching makes hypocrites out of a good many Americans, and it misses a very important fact that many of us have discovered. When the comedian Lenny Bruce was asked what he thought of pornography, he replied, "It helps!"

Only a small percentage of partners who view pornography will cheat on their partner. With so many people viewing sex, it has become a norm. At one time it was believed that only really "sick" and mentally ill people masturbated. Alfred Kinsey's research disproved that misinformation. He found that most men masturbated. These were men who were responsible, decent people. They held important positions in the workplace and demonstrated maturity and accountability.[3] I suspect there is currently a lot of negative misinformation about pornography. History may be repeating itself!

The subject of pornography is very difficult to discuss. Many people are very critical of the idea of watching porn. There are professional psychologists who condemn porn as being not only destructive of marital relationships but also an addiction that can totally ruin a person's life. The sexual addiction movement continues to gain momentum. It seems that any male getting caught either having affairs or just viewing porn is tagged as being "sexually addicted." Although sexual addiction is currently a popular topic and referred to as the new psychological pandemic, many professionals are critical of the idea of sexual addition. It is interesting to note that the American Psychiatric Association does not recognize either Internet addiction or sex addiction as a legitimate category for their fifth edition of the *Diagnostic and Statistical Manual of Mental Disorders*, published in 2013.[4] After a thorough study of the idea of sexual addiction, some of the brightest minds in the mental health field concluded that there was no legitimate research to support its existence.

THE SEXUAL ADDICTION CONTROVERSY

Patrick Carnes, PhD, has identified sexual addiction and addiction to Internet porn as very destructive addictions that, according to his view, is ruining thousands of lives and destroying marriages.[5] He is not alone in his view. Most religions, especially Christian conservatives and fundamentalists, Catholics, Mormons, Muslims, and Orthodox Jews, and some far-to-the-right feminists do not support any viewing of pornography. However, you should be aware that these groups also do not support gay rights, gay marriage, comprehensive sex education, contraception, freedom of choice about abortion, the morning-after pill, the right to sexual autonomy, which includes sex before marriage, and the practice of masturbation. In addition, they consistently have a problem with feminism. It seems that those who are against viewing anything erotic or explicit are also negative about most other sexual issues. For them, sex is dangerous. They support censorship of art, books, movies, and plays.

Criminologists and social workers that study and work with criminals and sex offenders dismiss pornography as a causal factor.[6] They see early childhood experiences, the cultural social structure they come from, brain physiology, and mental illness as the causal factors.[7] Even Dr. Carnes recognizes that there are established mental health categories that could explain the behavior of many clients he diagnoses as "sexually addicted." He states: "During the assessment process, a therapist needs to rule out all other possible diagnoses that may be complicating the clinical presentation. Common ones include antisocial personality disorder, narcissistic personality disorder, bipolar disorder, delusional disorder (erotomanic subtype), cognitive disorders (e.g., brain injury) paraphilias, and impulse control disorders. Common co-morbid conditions include substance abuse dependence, eating disorders, and ADHD."[8] Would that not almost entirely cover what he wants to diagnose as sexual addiction? What he calls a "sexually addicted" client could be suffering from antisocial personality disorder or narcissistic personality disorder.

We know that a small percentage of people have a condition called "compulsive sexual behavior." Others have compulsive gambling behavior, compulsive drinking, or compulsive hoarding or collecting. These unfortunate people ruin their marriages and their lives because they have a mental or psychological disorder. It is not that sex addicts them and then ruins them; they ruin their own lives because of a mental condition they cannot control. They do not even understand it. Carnes describes the extreme cases to make his point, but the behavior he describes is not unlike what happens to the life of anyone with a personality disorder or other mental illness.[9] Sexual addictions are talked about in our culture as if they were a pandemic disease spreading throughout society, ruining lives and marriages. However, this is not the situation. To the contrary, this represents a small minority of disturbed or immature people. The rest sounds like hype. There are millions of dollars being made from the sexual addiction movement. The reason so many social scientists and professionals are uncomfortable with this movement is their concern that this sexual addiction crusade is a repeat of history. Remember what was said about masturbation during the nineteenth century? Have we entered a neo-Victorian movement in American society? Are the judgments being made about pornography and sex just part of the negative sexual scripting by those who fear sexual freedom and sexual autonomy? Now that science has proved that masturbation is not harmful, is pornography the new target to re-pathologize? Dr. Marty Klein talks about people he calls "erotophobes." These people fear anything erotic as being sinful, harmful, or unhealthy.[10] Erotophobes present themselves as guardians of conventional morality. They have difficulty with sexuality and promote a negative sexual script as the sexual standard for society. They continually exaggerate, distort, misinform, even lie about sexual issues.

THE RESEARCH ON PORNOGRAPHY

When you look at the research on viewing pornography, you can find whatever you are looking to find. The research is confusing because it is so distorted and biased by false research designed to make porn menacing. There is voluminous "research" that is not research. It is created to appear to support what the negative sexual script erotophobes have been perpetuating for centuries. They create research with a bias toward supporting their bias! Real research is submitted for peer review in recognized university research journals. The research is described, and other research scientists can review how the research data was gathered and how it was interpreted. Other scientists can duplicate the research if they choose.

There is always some bias in all research, but some purported research is little more than propaganda. One well-known example is the research on the effects of pornography commissioned by President Ronald Reagan in 1986. This is often referred to as the Meese Commission Report, since President Reagan had Attorney General Edwin Meese chair it. This "research" produced some very negative views on pornography and recommended making it against the law. The Meese report was rejected by the scientific community, which observed that it was based on politics and not science. It was criticized because it lacked any scientific evidence to support its conclusion.[11]

A recent study on the effect of pornography on men by Dr. Simon Louis Lajeunesse, a researcher at the University of Montreal, Canada, found that all the men in the study supported equal rights for women. Pornography did not change their perception of women. Dr. Lajeunesse made a very poignant observation: "If pornography had the impact that many claim it has, you would just have to show heterosexual films to a homosexual to change his sexual orientation."[12] Other studies have concluded that men who watch pornography, compared to men who do not, are more empathic toward women and supportive of women's issues.[13] In other words, they like women!

Let us put aside the research on how harmful viewing pornography may or may not be. Here are some interesting facts that we do know. When we look at other cultures, it is apparent that pornography and violence against women may have no relationship at all. Denmark legalized all pornography in 1967; they had a 68 percent drop in sex crimes.[14] Japan legalized all pornography in 1972; from 1972 to 1995 rapes dropped from 4,677 per year to 1,500 per year. In the United States, rape has dropped 85 percent since 1973. That is despite the increased access to pornography. Research shows that between 1980 and 2000, states with the greatest Internet access also had the largest decrease of rape per capita. Alaska, Colorado, New Jersey, and Washington, which have the highest rate of access to Internet pornography, also had a 27 percent decrease in rape. The states with the lowest access to Internet porn (Arkansas, Kentucky, Minnesota, and West Virginia) had a 53 percent increase in rape. Remember that rape has dropped by

85 percent nationally, but it has increased where access to Internet porn is limited. [15]

WHAT IS PORNOGRAPHY?

America's Puritan and Victorian history, labels almost anything as pornographic. Nudity is pornographic. *Playboy* magazine shows mostly nude women. There are no penises. It is still condemned as pornographic. Americans are not to view anything that is naked, anything erotic. We are not supposed to view anything with sexual content. In America, those who are fearful of their sexuality define anything that can be sexually arousing as pornographic. They have censored classic art and rejected books with sexual content. They have banned books from libraries and bookstores. Some of these books are considered classic works, for example: *An American Tragedy, The Arabian Nights, The Art of Love, Confessions, Fanny Hill, Forever Amber, The Kama Sutra, Lady Chatterley's Lover, Lolita, Madame Bovary, Peyton Place, Tropic of Cancer, Women in Love,* and *Ulysses*. [16]

We are not to see sex, read anything that may be erotic, or even fantasize about sex. Essentially, we are not to be aroused by anything other than our spouse. We are to have no outlets for sexual expression other than sex with our married partner. The message is that sexual arousal is the sin. Most of our states do not allow comprehensive sex education out of misplaced fear that it would stimulate young adults to have sex before they marry.

This censorship of anything sexual may be explained by that corrupted lust passage (Matthew 5:27–28) in the Bible. We cannot look at nudity, not even if it is art, because it might create lustful thoughts! The message is that lust is immoral and sinful.

THE DIFFERENT KINDS OF PORNOGRAPHY

There are basically six kinds of pornography:

1. Erotica (sex) with violence
2. Erotica (sex) with a child or minor

3. Erotica (sex) with an animal
4. Erotica (sex) with abuse and degradation toward women or men (demeaning and degrading, but not violent pornography)
5. Nudity (naked men or women but no sex)
6. Erotica (sex) between two or more consenting adults with no abuse or degradation

Number 6 is what most people are watching. If a married couple filmed themselves having sex, that would be considered pornography in this culture. Could there possibly be some positive benefits to viewing consenting adult, nonviolent, non-degrading sex?

POTENTIAL BENEFITS TO WATCHING EROTIC VIDEOS

There can be some benefits to watching erotic videos.

Watching erotic videos can help desensitize you to sexual inhibitions, guilt, and fear. Through repeated viewing, erotic videos can help you become more comfortable with having sex and trying different positions and arousing techniques. Women more than men have difficulty becoming desensitized to erotica. Some men who come from an orthodox religious background also can have difficulty viewing erotica. They have received so many negative messages about being "moral" and "upright" that they fear erotic feelings. They are taught that lust is sinful and wrong.

Women receive considerable social conditioning to guard against ever behaving like a "slut" or a "whore." Of course, some would feel that only a slut or whore would expose her sexuality on a video for everyone to view. You can make love, but you cannot make erotica.

Erotic videos can teach you how to make erotica. It often takes repeated viewing to get comfortable with focusing on your own eroticism. Doing so can help you become more comfortable getting into an aroused state, which will ultimately give you more pleasure. If a woman wants to become orgasmic, she needs to learn how to surrender to erotic feelings, just like the men and women in the videos.

Porn stars can be excellent models for sexual freedom because they have completely disinhibited themselves. They are not afraid of deep erotic states. Study how they make erotica. Suspend judging them and instead posture as a student to learn from them. Remember, the desensitizing process is cumulative. You may have to make yourself watch the sex video over and over until you can relax and stop judging it. Then you can learn from it. Most people are so negatively scripted that they have a very difficult time seeing anything positive in pornography.

Erotic videos can be educational. Sometimes erotic videos are the only source of clear information on how to have good sex. They can demonstrate techniques on how to give and receive pleasure. Visual learning is one of the best sources for comprehension of almost anything. Studies have concluded that for some couples, viewing pornography improved their sex life and their marriage. One study in Australia surveyed more than one thousand porn users. It found that 90 percent of the viewers believed watching porn made them more attentive to their partners, more accepting of their sexuality, and less judgmental of body shapes. Those surveyed felt that viewing porn actually made their relationships and their marriages stronger. Couples who watch porn together often find that they can talk about their sexuality more freely.

Pornography can be a psychological aphrodisiac. Pornography stimulates the sexual center of the brain, which helps move a person from everyday reality to erotic reality. Erotic videos can get your mind focused on sex. They can be a part of foreplay and can heighten sexual excitement in preparation for intercourse.

Pornography can help the release of sexual tension. Erotic videos can be a wonderful sexual partner. They provide the means to have sex with yourself. They can also enrich sexual fantasy. Sexual fantasy induces arousal that moves you into an erotic state. This is helpful for reaching orgasm and releasing sexual tension. Often a person is feeling some sexual tension that is keeping him or her from concentrating. The person has difficulty focusing or even falling asleep. Imagine a scale of 1 to 10, with 10 being "reaching a climax" and 1 being "not feeling sexual." A person at 5 or 6 on the scale has enough sexual tension to feel uncomfortable but not enough to be able to relieve him- or herself. Pornography can stimulate us to a 10!

ARGUMENTS AGAINST PORNOGRAPHY

Pornography is sexist. One of the oldest arguments against pornography is that it makes sex objects out of women. Both men and women are "sports objects" in athletic competition, but nobody complains about that. Look at any magazine rack in the stores and you will see women models on the covers of the most popular magazines. Those models are clearly "objects."

It is interesting that some of the women who get so upset about making women sex objects in erotic videos buy magazines that objectify the women on their covers. It really is about sex. Both men and women are objects in modeling, in advertising, and in the fashion industry. In fact, cosmetics, hair styling, and fashionable clothing make objects out of everyone. The first thing we see about a person is the appearance of that person as an object.

The real issue for those who protest too much is their own discomfort over women being sexual and surrendering to their own erotic feelings. Has anyone who gets upset over women in porn videos ever considered that some women love sexual pleasure and have learned how to enjoy being erotic? Could some of the women in porn films be women who enjoy giving and taking sexual pleasure? How are women supposed to look when they are having sex? Some feminists think the sex act itself is degrading to women, even if it is with one's husband!

Porn movies are disgusting in the way they treat women. There is a wide variety of pornographic films on the market, and everyone needs to choose which films best suit his or her needs. You need to find what erotic films you are comfortable viewing. There are erotic films made by amateurs who are not professionals but a couple, often married, who decided to make a porn film. There is also "women's pornography," pornography made by women for women.

Some people are critical of erotic films because they think normal women do not have sex the way it is depicted in porn movies. While that may be true for most women, it is not true for all women. Some women do "make love" just like the women in the porn movies. There is very little that bothers these women about sexual activity. They are liberated from the negative sexual scripting in our culture. They are part of the 9.4 million women who view and enjoy pornography on their computers. Many more enjoy sexual stimulation from other sources, like books and magazines.

Pornography causes sexism and violence. Some very credible scientific research supports the view that sexism and violence against women are not caused by pornography.[17] Those social aberrations against women are caused by social structure, not by sex films. The history of killing women as witches was not caused by pornography. Making women cover themselves from head to toe and walk behind or be submissive to males is not caused by pornography. Blaming women for the downfall of all mankind as the descendants of Eve is not caused by pornography. Discriminating against women having positions of authority and power is not caused by pornography.

Women are discriminated against even where pornography is illegal. In the Middle East, women are discriminated against even though pornography is against the law. In some parts of the Middle East, women are not permitted to go to school or learn to read. Honor killings and blaming and arresting women who are raped are not caused by pornography. There is more violence toward women in American movies than you will see in most pornography. Slasher films, serial killer movies, the *Halloween* franchise, and the *Friday the 13th* films, along with a host of "thriller" movies in which women are raped, beaten, and killed, are not caused by pornography. Many women watch these "violence toward women" movies. They do not seem too bothered about sexism and violence toward women in the movies, but a porn movie becomes a big issue. They are really feeling discomfort with the lust being depicted. The negative scripting prevalent in our culture has conditioned them. It seems as though violence, killing, and rape are more acceptable in America than are lust and sex.

Porn movies are just distasteful. We pick and choose what movies we want to see at our local theaters. We should be equally selective about the erotic films we watch. There is a plethora of distasteful porn that many of us could never enjoy. We must sort out the erotic movies that fit our taste. A couple might consider making their own porn film to watch. The real issue is that in American culture, there does not seem to be any level of approval of explicit sex videos or even books that are erotic or sexual in nature.

Compared to men, many American women lack sexual desire and have profound difficulty reaching orgasm. How much of this problem is related to their negative conditioning about sex? The fact that so many married women's sexual interest varies so much from their male counterparts contributes to and inspires the male interest in pornography. Wives who lack an interest in sex can also be a contributing factor to male infidelity. It is also probable that getting rid of all porn would result in increased marital infidelity.

HOW MEN MANAGE SEXUAL FRUSTRATION

For heterosexual men, sexual fulfillment comes from having sex with a woman and from having sex with themselves. For most men, pornography is helpful to their reaching fulfillment. Most heterosexual men like looking at women. They also like looking at women having sex. What they find exciting about two women having sex is seeing both women in a sexual state of arousal and looking at their female bodies. A woman's arousal will arouse a man.

Most men find that pornographic or erotic material helps them ease their sexual frustration. Fantasy sex releases sexual tension and gives them pleasure. Men often use the erotic state as a great escape! They crawl into porn as if it were a comforting womb that protects them from all the frustration, threat, and stress of everyday reality. What would men feel if there was no porn available? Given that most men have pornographic minds, they would create their own fantasy world.

Pornography is of little interest to the minority of men who seem to lack sexual desire. They just do not have a strong sexual passion for women. Men who have strong orthodox religious beliefs against pornography and masturbation, abstain or participate very little in these erotic experiences. Often those men who make the loudest moral protest are the ones having the most difficulty with sex.

MALES AND SEXUAL PERFORMANCE

There are some serious issues for men regarding performance anxiety. Women can have sex just by "opening the gate." Even if they cannot self-lubricate, they can use commercial lubricants. The male has to get an erection, but that is not enough; he must keep that erection for a certain length of time. But that is not enough either. He must also be able to release, have an orgasm, and then go flaccid. Some men use Viagra, Cialis, or Levitra because they have health conditions that keep them from getting an erection without it. Many men who do not really need erection drugs use them because they have performance anxiety about getting and keeping an erection. While women need a feeling of emotional connection, men are worried about their performance and sexual functioning. Unlike women, most men reach an orgasm almost every time they have sex, but that does not necessarily mean they have performed well with their partners. Most men want their partner to enjoy having sex with them. They want it to be pleasurable for her. While women would like to hear "I love you" after sex, they usually hear "Did you come?" Men are more focused on how they performed than how they feel about their partner.

Men can and most often will experience some sexual dysfunction during their lifetime. That is obvious by the large sale of erectile dysfunction medication. Many men still are concerned about the size of their penis. The average male penis is about five inches in length when erect. Some males are as large as seven or eight inches, but not many have a penis much larger. The diameter of the average penis is approximately one and a half to two inches. A woman's vagina can accommodate almost any diameter penis, but the average woman's vaginal canal is only about four inches long. If a man's penis is too long, he can cause pain for the woman if his thrusting bangs his penis against her cervix. When this happens, it is like "kicking" her ovaries and she will feel a cramp-like pain. If a man's penis is too large for his female partner, he will have to shorten his stroke, have her mount him on top so she can adjust the stroke, or use the anterior position, which can better accommodate his larger penis.

Men can also have difficulty in climaxing too soon. The average male will come after stroking for about three to five minutes. The average woman needs between eight and ten minutes of stroking to reach satisfaction. This creates a problem for many couples. Men need to learn how to last longer, and women need to learn how to come faster. It is important for couples to spend more time with foreplay, which will make it easier for the female to come more quickly. Men who come too soon more than 50 percent of the time need to seek sex therapy to remedy the problem. Men who have difficulty releasing also should seek help, as should those who are too focused on performance.

There are no nerve endings in the vagina that provide sexual feeling.[18] Some nerve endings can provide some feeling in the first two inches of the vaginal opening, right behind the vaginal muscle. If a woman has a G-spot, she can have some erotic feeling in the first inch or two of her vaginal opening. Therefore, penis size really is not that important. If your female partner is attracted to you and likes you, she will be satisfied with your penis. Most men want their female partner to enjoy sex with them. Some consider satisfying their female partner to be a large part of their own sexual fulfillment.

The great majority of men enjoy pleasure in sex and have little trouble reaching orgasm. When males experience sexual dysfunction, it is very troubling for them. Being able to perform is more important than being emotionally connected to their partner. Could a woman's need to feel close and connected to her partner be so important because she is not comfortable having sex just for her own erotic pleasure? Does she need some higher purpose or value other than erotica? For males, sex is often about tension release. They feel strong sexual tension and feel pleasure when they can release that tension in orgasm. Being in an erotic state is so different from being in a normal everyday state of reality. Reaching orgasm is not difficult for most men because they have learned how to surrender to erotica and enjoy the pleasure of being in an erotic state. Remember, there are no books written on how a man can have an orgasm. Books on how to have an orgasm are written for women, who seem to have the most difficulty with it.

HOW TESTOSTERONE CONTRIBUTES TO THE DIFFERENCE IN MALE AND FEMALE DESIRE

There is another contributor to the difference in sexual desire in most men compared with most women. Both women's and men's bodies produce androgen. Androgen produces testosterone. It is the testosterone in both the female and the male that creates sexual desire. A minority of women produce higher levels of testosterone; these women tend to feel great desire almost like that of men. However, most males produce twenty to forty times more testosterone than the majority of women.[19] This could explain why males desire so much sex and why they have so much sexual frustration. It would also explain why there is such a difference in sexual interest between men and women.

THE MALE DIFFICULTY WITH GETTING EMOTIONALLY CONNECTED

For most men, sex is more a physical experience than an emotional one. For most women, sex is more of an emotional experience. They want to feel connected to their male partner. They often complain that sex with their partner is so mechanical that they feel like a prostitute. Because of their cultural conditioning, men often have difficulty with expressing their emotions and feelings. It may be that some of the issues from the nonsexual part of a couple's relationship come to the foreground in sex. If men knew how to make "emotional love" to their partners out of the bedroom, would this feeling of lack of connection in sex exist? Alternatively, if women were more focused on erotica and the sexual sensations of their own body, would emotional connection be such an important issue for them?

7

MARRIAGE

Creating a Deep Sexual and Emotional Connection

When you read the story of David and Lisa in chapter 6, what did you feel about them? Could you see trouble in their future together? Did you think David might eventually have an affair? If so, would you blame it on the pornography David is watching? Would you blame it on Lisa's negative sexual script? Would you blame David for not being more direct and aggressive in communicating his needs to Lisa? What does Lisa need to become aware of? What is David not aware of? Does Lisa understand that she is setting all the rules for their sexual relationship? Does she understand that she and David are in very different places regarding sex? Does she realize that the sexual boundaries she has set are so restrictive that they are inspiring David to think more of other women? Does David have any idea that if he is ever given the option, he will probably get involved with someone else? Is he aware that he sometimes relates to Lisa as though she were his mother? That at other times he relates to her as nothing more than a sex object?

David has no idea of how to make "emotional love" to Lisa. He never really connects with her, and on some level, she knows that. David and Lisa never fight. If they ever start to fight, they end it very quickly. They end it before either of them can resolve or learn anything. David withdraws and becomes quiet. Lisa yells, starts to cry, and runs to the bedroom, slamming the door behind her.

THE ELEPHANT IN THE LIVING ROOM

David and Lisa communicate on the surface. They keep their interaction hygienic and banal. They do not talk about what really matters. They both avoid what is uncomfortable and unpleasant. The rule is to always be positive about everything. Both think they have a good marriage. They would both say that they love each other. They might even celebrate the fact that they never fight! Do you see the "elephant in the living room" they will not talk about?

At first meeting, any competent marriage counselor would recognize immediately that this marriage has serious problems. The night Lisa caught David looking at pornography on his computer actually was a very fortunate event for the health and future of their marriage. This event motivated them to dive deeper into the repressed issues in their relationship. How can David and Lisa have a good marriage when they do not know how to talk to each other? There are no good marriages without good communication. Relevant issues are not going to be addressed if you do not have the skills of communication. But communication requires more than just talking and listening; it needs to be more than making noise at each other. The basic structure of an interaction between two people is that one talks and the other listens. That may seem simple enough, but when you have emotional issues and are upset, it is difficult to listen. Especially if you are being criticized, you instinctively want to defend yourself. When you hear a couple talking and you hear both their voices at the same time, you know nobody is listening. In communication, couples need to take turns listening and talking.

Why does David withdraw from Lisa and repress his self-expression? There are several possibilities: He may not know what to say; he may know what he wants to say but is afraid to say it for fear it will upset Lisa; he may withhold his self-expression because he is angry at Lisa and chooses not to respond to her. When he is angry with her, he may "stonewall" her and keep quiet as a form of punishment. Being unresponsive is often referred to as the "silent treatment." Another reason David may not express himself has to do with his fear of intimacy. He fears that by expressing his feelings, he is making himself a target for Lisa's criticism and putdowns. He fears she will make him look stupid.

What he wants to say may be so personal that he feels embarrassed to say it.

WHAT COUPLES NEED TO LEARN

One of the first things David had to learn was that unless he told Lisa what he was feeling, nothing could be worked out. If David did not know what he was feeling, he would need some help from a therapist to learn to identify his feelings. However, in his case he knew what he felt but was afraid to express it.

One of the first things Lisa had to learn was that she does not listen to David when he tries to tell her what he feels. Whenever she hears something negative, she exits the transaction, so it cannot become an interaction. Even her crying was a defense against listening to David because it always stopped the communication, especially when her crying was accompanied by anger.

I have heard many women complain that their husbands will not talk to them. What these women often do not recognize is that whenever their husband does try to talk, they cut him off before he can finish a sentence. The husband is never able to complete his thought before the wife is reacting to it with a defensive response. This usually either shuts the husband up or makes him get defensive and dismiss his wife. Then his voice gets louder and his wife yells at him to stop yelling at her.

WHY MEN FIND IT HARD TO LISTEN TO WOMEN

Men do not listen to women. I have seen many couples where the husband thinks they are coming in for marriage counseling, but the wife is actually finished with the marriage and wants to talk about divorce. When the wife tells him she is leaving, the husband is always surprised. Although his wife had warned him and told him consistently that she was going to leave, he never heard or listened to her. Why could he not hear? So many men in America just do not take women seriously.[1] Countless times, I have watched men try to talk their female partner out of her feelings. It usually makes their partner more angry and defensive, or, worse yet, she just gets quiet and stops talking. If women are supposed to be submissive to men, why should men listen to them? According to the Bible, wives are supposed to submit to what their husbands say.

Remember, this is a patriarchal culture. Some of the Bible verses quoted in chapter 2 teach that a woman "shall have no authority over a man"; that women should "keep silent"; that wives should defer all decisions to their husband.

Sweden has the most equality between men and women. Women earn the same pay as men in every occupation in Sweden. In addition, the country has the same balance of men and women in almost all occupations.[2] Sweden treats prostitutes humanely. Instead of arresting them, the government provides funding to retrain them for a different career if they want one.[3] This is not true in America, where patriarchy and the Puritan-Victorian distrust of women still rule. Unlike in most developed Western countries, prostitutes in America are arrested, fined, and/or jailed. Their "Johns" are usually left alone.

The Catholic Church claims to support women's rights and women's equality, but have you ever seen a female Catholic priest, bishop, cardinal, or pope? Have you ever compared a nun's status with the power and status of the males who administrate and control everything in the Church?

Those who promote the negative sexual script think of women as the weaker gender. Women cannot really be trusted to hold the highest office in America. Unlike many other countries, America has never elected a female president. What countries have elected a female president or prime minister? Here are just a few: Great Britain, India, Portugal, Bolivia, Israel, Iceland, Norway, the Netherlands, the Philippines, Yugoslavia, Central African Republic, Finland, Panama, Mongolia, Bermuda, Switzerland, Ireland, Canada, France, Nicaragua, Pakistan, Germany, New Zealand, Poland, and Malta.[4]

The business world is also illustrative of denying women power. In America, among the top Fortune 500 companies, women hold only approximately 20 percent of upper management positions.[5]

HOW WE TREAT FEMALE PROSTITUTES

While we are looking at our cultural attitudes toward women, consider how we treat female prostitutes. Prostitution is against the law everywhere in America except Nevada. In all the other forty-nine states, prostitutes are arrested, fined, even jailed. They are treated with complete contempt. Most Americans are not aware of all the countries where not only is prostitution legal, but it is against the law to be a pimp. In many other countries, pimps, not prostitutes, are arrested. These countries include Brazil, Bulgaria, Canada, Finland, France, Germany, Greece, Israel, and Sweden.[6] These countries do not punish women as though they were Eve, as we do in America. Being a prostitute or a pimp is legal in many countries, including Costa Rica, the Czech Republic, Denmark, Hungary, Italy, Kenya, Mexico, the Netherlands, New Zealand, Norway, Romania, Spain, Switzerland, England, Russia, Singapore, Austria, and Australia.[7] It is not that countries with legalized prostitution have no religion. They simply recognize that most women become prostitutes to keep from being impoverished. They do not treat them as though they were Eve!

America is still a very patriarchal culture. Women are still discriminated against and disparaged by men. Their feelings and opinions are still discounted. We still have the double standard. Being sexually active somehow makes men manly. Sexually active women, on the other hand, are often referred to as sluts and whores. Some men feel they do not have to respect women and feel justified in discriminating against them. They can feel comfortable exploiting women because they view them as the weaker sex. They often discount what women feel because they think women are irrational. In truth, they feel superior to women. There are certainly exceptions, especially with the younger men who have grown up with feminist mothers, but generally husbands have difficulty listening to their wives and accepting what they are saying.

Another factor contributes to men having difficulty listening to women. As little boys, we grew up with a mother who did most of the caretaking and parenting. Our mothers called us to come in to take a nap or to wash up for dinner. Our mothers did almost everything for us. They did our laundry, changed our sheets, made our bed, fed us, advised us, warned us, told us what we could and could not do. Most males heard their mother's voice more than any other person's while they were growing up and built up an immunity to it. We were having so much fun playing with peers that when we heard Mother calling us home, we either pretended we did not hear her or ran and hid from her. When she caught up with us, she was angry and scolded us. By the time we were teens, we stopped listening to our mother's fears, worries, and warnings. A few years later, when we married, we unconsciously slipped into the same psychological posture with our wife that we had formed with our mother.

Men often feel that women worry too much, whine too much, get too emotional and irrational. Then there are all the stories of women and their monthly periods, which make them so irrational. Husbands stop listening, and when they do listen, they do not take anything their wife says seriously. In fact, they discount whatever she says simply because it is coming from a woman. That connection between mother and wife is close enough to tune out the wife as if she were the mother.

John Gottman's research verifies that men who do not allow their wives' feelings and opinions to influence them have higher levels of marital dissatisfaction.[8] It should be noted here that men are as moody as women. They don't often cry, but they do withdraw, shut down, and clam up. They get "bitchy" and sarcastic. Why? Testosterone. Men are dealing with sexual tension, and it makes them as moody as or, in some cases, moodier than any female during her time of the month. Men just handle it differently. They stonewall or yell, just get angry, or withdraw and become depressed.

LEARNING TO COMMUNICATE EFFECTIVELY

What have David and Lisa learned from their marriage counselor? They learned that when they are going to talk about their relationship issues, they have to agree that they will follow some important rules:

1. Set a time and time limit for their conversation. When the agreed-upon time runs out, they should renegotiate it.
2. Agree that no one exits the conversation and runs from the interaction.
3. Take turns listening and talking. No one talks at the same time as the other. If one of them cuts the other off before he or she is

finished, the one being cut off tells the other, "Let me finish; you are cutting me off." They should not proceed further until the person who was talking regains the floor. Cutting your partner off will create defensiveness, which usually takes the form of your partner cutting you off in return.

4. Do not attack their partner's self-esteem. No labeling or name-calling is allowed. David does not call Lisa a "bitch"; Lisa does not call David an "asshole" or a "prick."

5. Make "I" statements to each other rather than "you" statements. "You" statements, such as "You always think negatively about what I do," create defensiveness. Such statements sound parental. They sound as though you are the authority over the other person; you are right, and you have the truth. It is more helpful to state, "I feel that you think negatively about what I do." This allows the possibility that you may be wrong. You are not stating that this is definitely how it is; it is simply how you feel. But your feelings could change if your partner shows you how your feelings are not accurate.

All feelings are valid for the person who feels them. Lisa could complain, "I feel that you are too critical of me." David previously responded defensively: "I don't think that is true at all." What he learned in his therapy is that there must be some validity to Lisa's feelings or she would not have them. He has learned to listen to what she is saying and not to invalidate what she says she is feeling. When your partner makes a critical statement about you, it is helpful—and wise—to first consider, "this could be true if my partner feels it."

ADDRESSING THE ISSUES THAT MATTER

So, now that we have David and Lisa understanding how to communicate, what are the issues they need to address?

Lisa wants to talk about the lack of connection she feels with David. She feels that most of the time he is preoccupied. She feels that he does not tell her what he feels or even what is on his mind. She has observed that when a friend of his calls him on the phone, he talks with a spontaneity that he never does with her. She feels he never tells her that he loves her unless she says it first, and then it does not sound like he really means it. Although she does almost all the cooking and cleaning, she never feels that David appreciates what she does. She works in the marketplace, and she works in their home. She does his laundry, folds it, and puts it in his drawer. She willingly does almost anything he asks her to do for him, but she rarely receives a thank-you. She wants him to do more around the house. She feels they really do not do anything together. When they do, she feels she must always be the one to initiate it. While she is reporting this, she is holding back her tears. It is obvious that when she thinks about how David treats her, she is unhappy and lonely in her marriage to him.

It is easy to guess what David wants to address: sex! David is like most men. Sex is one of the most important issues in his life. It is important because he desires it so much and because he feels so much sexual frustration. He is attracted to Lisa's body and likes having sex with her, but he does not like her inhibitions and the control she maintains throughout their sexual experience. She dictates what they can and cannot do. She also gets to determine when and where they will have sex. David does not believe she really has orgasms. After having sex with her, he always asks whether she came or not. He says she never seems to ever let go and come. Lisa always says she did, but David never believes her.

BECOMING A MORE EROTIC WOMAN

Lisa's marriage counselor recommended that she read Dr. Lonnie Barbach's excellent book *For Yourself: The Fulfillment of Female Sexuality*. Although written back in the 1960s, this is probably the best book ever written for women on the subject of masturbation; the information is still valid. It was written for women to help them become desensitized to the negative sexual script that condemns having sex with oneself. Once a woman has worked through the negative messages about masturbation, she can gain all the benefits discussed in chapter 3. After some needed education about reaching orgasm, Lisa climaxed for the first time.

Lisa started a completely new sex life with herself. Experiencing this pleasure and enjoyment gave new meaning to her life. She was learning how to enjoy her body. Giving herself private pleasure had a surprising effect on her. She started to like her body more, and with that discovery, she started liking herself more. She would tell David, "I like me, and I like my body." She now realized how enjoyable her body was to her. Her spirit and her body developed a new friendship through her acceptance and approval of masturbation.

As Lisa continued to stimulate herself and reach orgasm, other things began to happen. She started to change the way she dressed. Lisa had previously dressed like a "plain Jane." Now she started to dress more sensually: a touch more cosmetics, a bit more jewelry, clothes that fit a bit tighter, a different bra that didn't try to hide her breasts, and shoes with a touch of sensuality. She became more conscious of feeling sensuous. For the first time in her life, she felt in touch with her sexuality. Her mind was connected to her body; her body connected to her mind.

She did more. She started reading books that were clearly erotic in nature. First she started with the classics that had been banned by the negative sexual script promoters. She read *Lady Chatterley's Lover*; then she read *Lolita*. She found erotic literature stimulating. She read *Fifty Shades of Grey*. She was developing a sexual fantasy life, which was helping her sexual relationship with herself. It was also helping her sexual relationship with David. She rented some pornography films. She asked David to make a recording of the kinds of erotic scenes she found stimulating. This became a custom film of her own, with the kind of erotica that helped turn her on. By copying only what appealed to her, she could skip the boring material. She went online and discovered there was pornography for women. She found porn movies made by women for women. She even put some porn scenes on her iPhone so she could conveniently start the shift from everyday reality to erotic reality.

Lisa fully owned her sexuality. She was integrating her sexuality with her mind and her body. She started risking the use of erotic language. Using such language was a risk because she had always followed the script that "good girls don't talk like that." She started to challenge all those negative messages she had been told. Once when starting to make love with David, she said, "Fuck me." Then she said, "Let me feel your cock." Then she said, "Put your cock in me and make my cunt feel good." She realized how the use of erotic language was freeing her. She could move her body more freely as she let go of the negative scripting and surrendered to her lust feelings. As she focused on her sexual sensations, she found herself moving her body to increase the erotic feeling.

As Lisa fell increasingly into the erotic state she had often experienced while masturbating, she began to move her hips and pelvis in rhythm to David's stroking. She was not having sex; she was fucking! She was not making love with David; she was "screwing" him! She was "making erotica." She felt her passion increase to a place where she was hardly conscious of David because the sexual tension she was creating was totally taking over. She completely surrendered to her feelings of lust. She felt a profound sexual tension and then a flood of pleasure, which seemed to weld her mind and body together. She could feel pelvic contractions that were involuntary. With each contraction, she felt a surge of pleasure and a release of all tension. She felt so good. She was now able to return to David, who had released just after she had. She enjoyed herself so much. She felt a deep love for David for participating in her pleasure. She told him softly, "I just love fucking you." David did not have to ask her if she had come. He had felt her contractions and heard her moans of pleasure. All David said was, "God, I love you!" They held each other very tightly.

THE MONOGAMOUS SLUT-WHORE PLEASURE

As their sex life improved, David found his interest in pornography declining. He had never felt so turned on to Lisa as he was now. Often they would view twenty minutes of porn just to help them shift from everyday reality to erotic reality. When Lisa was not available, David would sometimes watch some porn and have sex with himself. Sometimes when David was not available, Lisa would watch some porn and have sex with her self. Lisa had lost her fear of being an erotic woman. She had come to the realization that she had become a "whore." She was a "slut." If a woman who is a slut and a whore is a woman who enjoys having sex and is sexually active, then Lisa is a slut and a whore. If it also means that she has sex with lots of men, then Lisa is what I would call a "monogamous slut and whore." When some hostile male calls a woman a whore, instead of being offended by that antiquated Victorian label, why not just respond, "And you are such an uptight, hostile prick that no whore would want to fuck you!"

Remember, there is in David what is in all men, and there is in all men what is in David. If Lisa can be turned on to David, then she can be turned on to other men. If she could not be turned on to other men, she could not be turned on to David because he is a man. The core of her attraction is to maleness. She is also "polymorphous perverse." She can be turned on by other men. She is also turned on by music and art. She can be turned on by nature and soft candlelight. She has integrity. She keeps her commitments. No matter how she is aroused, she has committed herself to fulfill all her sexual feelings with herself or with David. She is a "monogamous slut and whore." Lisa is not afraid of those words anymore. She is not ashamed that she is sexual. In fact, she feels good knowing she has so much "pussy power." Her sexuality has empowered her like she has never known. Her fear and inhibition have declined. She is now in control of her sexuality. She has never loved herself more. She has never felt so free to be herself. She can feel her power and confidence as a female who has integrated her body with her mind. Lisa now has her "MSW," and she finds those words utterly laughable.

DATING AND RELATING

After David and Lisa got married, they stopped dating. Couples should never stop dating, no matter how busy they become. In fact, many of the things they did in their courtship should have been carried into their marriage. They had fun when they were courting. Every week was full of dates. They made time to be with each other. They hiked beautiful trails, biked for miles, visited the zoo regularly. They fished; they went to concerts; they met for picnics in the park; they gave parties and went to parties; they went swimming; they went to movies; they took trips. They were constantly planning dates with each other.

Now they have been married for five years and do very little together. David was the one who did not want to go anywhere. He always complained that he was too tired from work to do anything. Once a week he would have beers with some male friends. Most of the time when he was at home, he would just sit and watch sports on television. David never realized how non-intimate he was with Lisa. He had to face some of the dark truth about himself. He did not even think of doing anything to inspire Lisa to want to open the gate and have sex with him. He knew how to make love to her sexually, but he had no idea how to make love to her emotionally. Most of the time, he never really looked at her. He never really studied who she was as a person and a life partner. He did not know the color of her eyes. He did not know her favorite food or her favorite music. He knew hardly anything about what she suffered as a child. He had no idea about what would make Lisa happy or excited. He had forgotten much of what he did know, like the fact that Lisa enjoyed dancing. They had actually met at a dance, but they had not been dancing in the five years since they had married.

An example of David's lack of relating to Lisa was demonstrated on her last birthday. David bought her flowers, a genuine pearl necklace, some expensive perfume, and a nice card that was signed, "Love you, David." When he gave the gifts to Lisa, she looked at it all and became very solemn. She started to cry; she threw the flowers at him, followed by the pearls and the perfume. She then screamed, "For the past year I have been asking you to build some bookshelves in the basement, and you kept telling me we couldn't afford the building materials. I do not want pearls and perfume. I want you to make me some bookshelves!" She then ran down the hall into the bedroom, slammed the door, threw herself on the bed, and sobbed.

If David had been listening to Lisa—if he had been tuned into her— he would have built her some bookshelves for her birthday. Because she felt David never listened to her, she reacted emotionally. She knew he still did not know who she was after eight years together. It was the last straw. She sobbed in hurt and frustration.

MEN NEED TO LEARN ABOUT CONNECTING

David had much to discover from his counseling. He learned that he needed to get to know who he was living with. He could start this process by forgetting about getting her to have sex with him. Instead, he learned to watch what she did when she was home. He started to listen in on her phone conversations; he paid attention to how she met and greeted people. He started to get interested in what she felt about things such as her family, her friends, the news in the paper and on television, how she felt about him and their relationship. When she was quiet, he started asking her what she was thinking. He established contact time with her.

Contact time involves setting dates to be alone together. It can be as simple as having coffee together or a glass of wine on the patio; playing cards or dominoes or board games together ritually. Board games can be relaxing and create an opportunity for chitchat, which can lead a couple to discuss deeper, more meaningful issues and needs. Couples need ritualized contact time in which they get together at the same time on a regular basis, such as going to lunch once a week, having coffee together every morning, watching a television program they both like. It is most important to make time daily to sit and talk together about how they are feeling about their relationship. It can be just before they go to bed or while they are in bed. It can be as soon as they are together after work. Contact rituals are absolutely one of the most important components of having a close and emotionally intimate relationship.

THE PROCESS OF CONNECTING AND DISCONNECTING

In all relationships, there is a constant connecting and disconnecting process. We may fall asleep feeling close to our partner, but even sleep separates us so that in the morning we wake disconnected. If you have coffee together with conversation, you may then be reconnected. If there is no time for that, even a genuine kiss and a felt hug can give you a sense of connection. When you both leave for work, you are disconnected. If you call or text your partner during the workday and talk together for a moment, you are connected again. When you return home and have no connecting ritual, you remain disconnected, perhaps for the entire evening. Couples need to become aware of the continual process of connecting and disconnecting, which is always operating in their relationship.

My observation is that men would have more sex with partners if they paid attention to more than just the sexual connection. They need to spend more time on the emotional and psychological connections. That is what David learned to do. Your partner is a sex object, but not just a sex object. Your partner is a person like you. Your partner has feelings about many issues in life. When you get to know your partner, you become connected emotionally and psychologically with your partner's feelings. When that happens, it is impossible for a third party to get between you and your partner. As David began to understand this and started to focus on getting to know who Lisa really was as a person, he started to realize how much he was enjoying the relationship. They were actually becoming friends. He started looking forward to seeing her when he came home from work. She felt the change in David. She could tell he was actually listening to her and interested in what she had to say. He was not judging her feelings nor undermining her opinions on issues. She could see that David liked talking to her. He liked listening to her. She actually started to feel that David loved her. It meant a lot to her when David finally built those bookshelves. It made her want to open the gate and open it wide.

ALWAYS HAVING YOUR PARTNER WITH YOU

When a couple is emotionally, psychologically, and spiritually connected, they feel their partner's spirit inside their own psyche. Even when you are apart, you can feel your connection to your partner. When Lisa is away from David, she feels his spirit; when David is away from Lisa, he feels her spirit. They are connected in a way that makes it impossible for another person to get in between them. Even though Lisa and David can feel attraction to someone else, they cannot act on that attraction because they feel as though their mate was standing right there with them. When you feel that emotional connection, it is as though your partner is always with you. Your partner's spirit is never completely out of your own feelings. You can be aware that you are attracted to someone else, but you cannot respond to that someone because you can feel the love you have for the person to whom you have committed your life. You can also feel your partner's love for you. It is nearly impossible to act on some physical attraction to another when you feel in love with your partner and are aware that your partner is in love with you. You would have to be a masochist, a narcissist, or a sociopath to mess up what is essentially a very good relationship.

David started spending more time with Lisa. She became his closest friend as well as his lover. During sex, he learned to take more time with foreplay. He learned not to move too fast. He took more time to arouse Lisa. He discovered what Masters and Johnson had learned in their sexual research with couples: If men who have difficulty getting a firm erection learn to stimulate their partner more, and to focus on their partner's arousal and excitement, they would be able to get erect without Viagra. When men look at porn, they focus on sexual excitement and arousal. They do not have to try and "think" an erection. They look at the sexual arousal of the woman in the porn and automatically get an erection. Now that Lisa knows how to get erotically aroused, and David has learned to take time to focus on arousing her, he doesn't have to worry about whether he will get erect or not.

David and Lisa have learned how to communicate; they have learned how to talk and listen; they have learned to suspend judgment on what their partner feels. They now date all the time. Their dating is actually a connecting ritual. No, they do not have to leave the house to go on a date. A connecting date can be on their patio, in their living room, or in their bed. They have learned how wonderful love is before sex and how wonderful it is after sex, but they know "making love" is really a cover-up for "making erotica" together for their pleasure. David and Lisa are no longer controlled by all those authorities, ministers, priests, rabbis, and institutions that keep reinforcing the negative sexual script. They are enlightened and liberated. That "elephant" in their living room is gone.

8

HOW ROMANCING CAN DEEPEN YOUR SEXUAL EXPERIENCE

Are you male? Unless you are one of the exceptions, your neurobiological brain wiring lights up around anything female. Are you female? Unless you are one of the exceptions, your neurobiological brain wiring lights up whenever you are around any living thing. That includes both human and animal.

I am speaking in generalities when I say that men are hypersensitive to sex and that sexual feeling is usually present in some form every day. Certainly there are women who are no different when it comes to feeling sexual tension. Most males find it easier to become more focused on having sex with their partner than trying to emotionally connect with her. Sexual tension becomes the foreground and connecting, the background.

The social conditioning women get to be chaste and sexually conservative teaches them to put sex more in the background and put connecting emotionally in the foreground. They learn very early from society, from parents, and from their peers that they cannot think or dress or behave like a "whore" or a "slut." The message to young girls is that any sexual behavior should be inhibited until they find some male that loves them. While they should wait till marriage, they can "fudge" a little if it is "love." While males can have sex just for tension release, females are more prone to have sex for love. Women are more relationship oriented. They need that love feeling or emotional connection in order to be sexual. That may explain why so many men feel sexually rejected by their wife or partner. It could also provide a clue as to why, after courtship, so many women lose a lot of their desire for sex.

I've had a lot of complaints from males in my office. One married man claimed to love his wife but said, "I just want to get laid by anybody!" He continued: "My wife has no desire for sex. I have been put off enough. I am going to find a call girl; I just have to think of myself. I won't tell my wife, but I need sex." Numerous males have told me that they get rejected and turned down so often that they just told their wife, "I am not going to initiate it any more, you tell me when you want to have sex." Most of these men turn to porn and masturbation to satisfy their sexual needs.

I've had wives ask their husbands why they never initiate sex anymore, and the answer they get is that their husband has gotten so many turndowns that he has given up trying. A lot of men feel that the woman controls their sexual relationship and makes all the rules about what they can and cannot do. For a lot of these men, watching porn and having fantasy sex with themselves is far less complicated than going through the maze set up by their wives.

I had a woman complain to me that her husband continually hounded her for sex. She said, "I just feel like he isn't interested in me. All he is interested in is sex. It feels so mechanical that I don't enjoy it." Some women feel their partners use them as a "tension release machine." They feel their husbands don't romance them or inspire them to want to have sex with them. Some men are so controlling and critical that they motivate their partners to have an affair with someone who treats them like an "OK" person.

Men need to learn how to express soft feelings with their female partner. I had a woman tell me that if her husband treated her like the men treat their partner in all those Viagra and Cialis ads, she would want to have sex with him. Oh, the woman who complained that her husband hounded her for sex all the time? I asked her to try an experiment. I told her to commit to having sex with her husband every single night for the next fourteen nights. She agreed to try it, and on the fifth night her husband said he was too tired!

This couple is in the minority; most women feel a need to emotionally bond or connect with most any living thing, particularly with people. Unwittingly, women create sexual tension for most men. As that tension builds, men feel a need to release that tension by having sex. That need trumps everything else in their lives!

ROMANTIC MARRIAGE: LOVING EACH OTHER

Tom and Jackie have been married for forty-one years. They have two adult children who no longer live with them. In the forty-one years they have been married, they have never done anything to profoundly hurt each other. There has never been any infidelity. There has never been a level of selfishness so great that it seriously scarred the relationship. Although they had some heavy fighting early in the relationship, they no longer really fight. They have differences from time to time, but they routinely discuss them and negotiate a settlement. There are times when they get emotional when discussing an issue they disagree on, but after expressing how they feel, they come together and negotiate an agreement. Their sexual relationship averages around twice a week, sometimes more and sometimes less. They plan dates every day. More than 90 percent of the time, they feel good with each other. They still feel the love and attraction they both had in the beginning of the relationship.

MAINTAINING THE ORIGINAL FEELING YOU HAD IN COURTSHIP

How have Tom and Jackie been able to keep the positive attraction for each other for forty-one years? If you study their relationship, you will observe how they have managed to do it.

1. They both have a lot of independence in their relationship. They do many things separately. Tom loves golf and plays weekly with some male friends. Jackie is not interested in golf, but she loves to walk, hike, and bike. She also loves to sew. Tom loves to watch sports on television. Jackie has women friends with whom she likes to go for coffee, and she often walks, talks, and bikes with them.

2. Since they both have careers, they have three bank accounts. One account is Jackie's, one is Tom's, and one is a joint account to which they both contribute to cover the joint costs of living. They rarely argue about money. They discuss any major purchase, and both contribute their share. From what I have described about them, can you identify some of the positive characteristics of their relationship?

3. They allow each other independence socially, psychologically, and financially. Neither is dominant. Tom is not the "head" of the household. There have always been two heads. They have managed to maintain a peer relationship for forty-one years! Jackie does not feel controlled by Tom, and Tom does not feel controlled by Jackie.

It was not like that in the beginning of their relationship. For the first five years of their marriage, they had horrendous fights. They were both strong, independent people. Tom was raised on the teachings of the negative sexual script. In his family, his father was the head of the household. In Jackie's family, her mother was the head of the household. Tom came from a traditional patriarchal family and Jackie from a matriarchal family. They fought for control. They fought to prove who was right.

It is difficult for couples to realize that "a fight to be right" is a dead-end fight. There are no winners. Whoever loses gets very resentful toward the partner who won. When a husband keeps losing to his wife, he will usually withdraw and stop talking to her. When a wife keeps losing to her husband, the first thing she usually does is stop having sex with him. It is almost impossible for a woman to have sex with someone toward whom she feels anger and resentment.

4. Tom and Jackie eventually realized that there were no winners with their fights. Their fighting did not resolve anything. Fighting just made them mad at each other and left them alienated. They discovered they were both right. Each of them had a piece of what was true, but neither would listen to the other's truth. They would each become fixated on their own truth and could not hear the truth in their partner's view. They finally started to really listen to each other with the purpose of understanding how their partner felt.

5. They know the rules of good communication—and they follow them. When one is talking, the other listens. Listening does not just mean keeping quiet. Listening is an active process of focusing on what your partner is saying and not thinking about what you want to say. You try to put your feet in your partner's shoes. Good listening involves empathy for what your partner is feeling and telling you. If your partner is telling you something that sounds critical, consider that there may be some truth in what he or she is saying!

6. Tom and Jackie have a very good sex life. It is above average for their ages and life stage. It is, of course, not frequent enough for Tom, but he compensates by having sex with himself. Sex is frequent enough that he does not feel that he is always being rejected. It is clear to him that Jackie likes sex and is a very sexual, sensual partner. He knows that she is a very erotic woman who likes to have sex, not just to please him but also to pleasure herself. Tom has learned how important foreplay is to Jackie. He takes plenty of time to make sure she is very turned on before they start intercourse. He has paid attention to how she likes to be pleasured. He has listened to what she has told him she likes. Usually, Jackie "comes" without much effort.

KEEPING YOURSELF AND YOUR RELATIONSHIP EROTIC

Jackie discovered masturbation when she was about twelve years old. She found her clitoris and massaged it regularly. Pleasuring herself to orgasm became a regular activity. It made her feel so good. It relaxed her. It connected her mind to her body. Masturbation gave her a positive feeling about her body. She had her first sexual experience with a boy when she was about sixteen years old. Her mother had told her about birth control and sent her to a class at Planned Parenthood so that she knew the importance of protecting herself. Her mother made certain Jackie had easy access to several methods of birth control. Her mother did not teach her abstinence until marriage; her mother taught her responsibility.

By the time she met Tom, Jackie was very experienced with her sexuality. She knew her body well and knew how to shift into erotic reality. Orgasm was never difficult for her. She has always enjoyed sex with Tom. Sometimes she will have sex with him just because she knows how important it is to him. Jackie knows how strong the sex drive is in males and has empathy for Tom's sexual frustrations. When she is just trying to please Tom, she often will not have an orgasm, even though he gets satisfied. Although she does not have an orgasm during these encounters, she still enjoys the physical closeness and giving pleasure to Tom. Jackie still enjoys masturbation. It is a real part of her sexual enjoyment, and her feeling of closeness to herself. Jackie likes feeling sensual. She dresses sensually and is comfortable talking about sex. Sometimes she enjoys sexually teasing Tom. She knows it turns him on. She has no shame about her body, and she lets Tom see her nude as much as she is able. She delights in knowing the power of her pussy.

Jackie loves being a woman. She enjoys being a sensual, sexual, woman. Knowing this gives her an erotic spirit that transcends what she weighs or the size of her breasts. Jackie knows she has something far more attractive than a perfect body. If Tom is in the room or comes into the room when she is dressing, she sometimes flashes a quick sexual pose at him. Sometimes when Tom comes home and she is sitting in a chair reading, she will lift her skirt, spread her legs, and then quickly go back to reading. She usually gets a hot kiss from Tom, and just like that, they are connected emotionally. She is sending him a message that "tonight is the night," but not right now; right now, "let's talk."

Sometimes when Tom is watching pornography, Jackie will look over his shoulder and make comments on how hot and sexy the women look and how the men are great studs. She will often tongue his ear or reach down into his crotch to feel his hard-on. If they come upon a strikingly beautiful woman when they are out in public, Jackie will point her out to Tom. She might say something like "Look at her, Tom; isn't she beautiful?" or "Look at her; isn't she hot?"

For Tom, just knowing that Jackie enjoys sex and that he enjoys having sex with her seems to lessen his sexual frustration. Although he does not get all the sex he would like, the quality of the sex he has with Jackie compensates for the lack of quantity. He knows that sex is good, and that fact curbs his interest in both pornography and other women he meets in the marketplace.

THE IMPORTANCE OF DATE PLANNING

Tom and Jackie are always planning dates together. A "date" for them is arranging any contact time for them to do something together. They may make a date to watch the NBA playoffs on Thursday night together. They may make a date to meet on the patio at 8:00 p.m. for a glass of wine. They make dates for a concert or a movie. They will make a date to play cards together.

For them, dating is planning time to be together. It does not have to be "going out," but occasionally they do go out. Most often, their date is stopping what they are doing independently and coming together. What is important is that they are planning contact time in every day. It is always something they are going to do together. Most of the time, they make dates just to talk. Sometimes they have "spontaneous dates," where one comes to the other and says, "Let's take a break together." Then they drop what they were doing independently and come together. Sometimes they make dates in the future for trips or concerts and put these dates on their calendars. Often during the week, they plan what they are going to be doing on the weekend. What is very clear is that Tom and Jackie have made their relationship a priority. Getting together for contact time is primary in their lives. There is not a day of the week they do not talk to each other.

THE LANGUAGE OF ENDEARMENT

There is something else that explains the close connection of Tom and Jackie. In the early years of their marriage, when they were having what seemed like constant power struggles, they went to a marriage counselor. The counselor taught them something that made a truly remarkable difference in their relationship. In fact, couples that learn what they have learned will feel an emotional intimacy the likes of which they have never known.

Have you ever considered that emotional intimacy has its own language? If you learn this language and use it in your communication, you will feel a closer bond. What is this language? I have called it "the language of endearment." The exchange of endearing language between couples creates a warm intimate feeling in their relationship. Endearing language is romantic language. It is the language of poets and lovers. If you focus on all the right features of your partner—the personal qualities you saw when you first met, the qualities of your partner you still appreciate—and start to verbalize that information to your partner, you will be endearing your partner. If your partner reciprocates so that it is a mutual exchange, you will be making emotional love to each other. It will create a feeling of closeness. What makes the language of endearment so powerful is the fact that it is a form of

emotional reinforcement. Couples who learn this form of reinforcement have a feeling of connectedness in their relationship that is almost
impossible for someone else to break. Let me illustrate.

Tom and Jackie are sitting in their living room reading on a Saturday
morning.

Jackie: "Tom, I just love being with you like this. Isn't it nice just to
be so relaxed together reading?"

Tom: "Yeah, this is really nice. I just love being with you."

Jackie: "I feel so lucky to have someone like you in my life."

Tom: "I feel the same way. You're a fine person. A real sweetheart."

Jackie: "You are such a love. Where did I ever find you? I am so
lucky to have a man like you."

Tom: "I feel I am so lucky to have a woman like you. I've never met
anyone like you. You are so responsible and loving to me, and I
appreciate all that you do for me and for us."

Jackie: "You've been such a great father to our kids. You're a lot of
fun, and you make me laugh so much. I know that I am blessed to
have someone so wonderful in my life."

Tom: "You are very beautiful. I am so attracted to you. I love your
body and appreciate that you enjoy having sex. I don't know what I
would do without you. I just love you."

Jackie: "You are so handsome!" Jackie gets up out of her chair and
comes to Tom. "I want to hug you." They hug and kiss; Tom fondles
her, and they hold each other for a minute. Then Jackie speaks:
"What do you want to do tonight?"

Tom: "You mean besides having sex? Let's dress up and go to dinner. I love going out with a hot woman!"

Jackie: "And I love going out with a handsome man. I love you so
much."

Tom: "Jackie, you are just great. I really appreciate all that you do and all that you handle in our life. I am so lucky to be married to a mature and loving woman."

The "language of endearment" is always complimentary language. Whatever you say when making emotional love to each other, it is always a validation of the relationship and your partner. The focus is totally on what is right about your partner and your relationship together. You never mention any "negatives" when you are being endearing. The interaction between you and your partner should always be positive when you are making emotional love to each other.

Tom: "That was such a great dinner you made last night. I am so lucky to be married to a chef!"

Jackie: "You are such a dear; I am so lucky to have a man like you for a partner."

Tom: "Jackie, I just love you so much. You are really something else. You are just incredible. I am married to a great person. You are the light of my life. You make my life wonderful."

Jackie: "I really appreciate how you fixed that dripping faucet. How lucky I am to be married to a man that can fix things. You are just incredible."

Tom: "Well don't think I didn't notice that you changed the sheets on the bed. You do so much around here. And don't think I don't appreciate all that you do. I am a lucky man to have someone like you."

ROMANCING IS A CELEBRATION OF YOUR PARTNER

Couples can use their own creativity to find ways of validating and affirming their partner. Whatever you say does not have to be rational or logical. Remember, the "language of endearment" is not science; it is poetry. Poets have a license to say things that in fact are not true. A poet can say, "The clouds laughed, the trees danced, and the grass smiled."

We all know clouds do not laugh, trees do not dance, and grass does not smile. Such talk communicates a joyful celebration of nature. It communicates a state of happiness.

When you are making emotional love to your partner, remember that it is about poetry, not logic and reason. Jackie could say to Tom, "I couldn't live without you." In fact, such a statement is not true. If Tom died, Jackie would no doubt fall in love with some other man, rebuild her life, and continue living. That is not the point. Jackie is being a poet. She is expressing how deeply in love she is with Tom and how connected she feels to him. She is affirming how much he means to her. Tom tells Jackie, "Being with you is like being in heaven. When I am with you, the stars shine brighter, my heart wants to dance, and I just feel so good being with you."

As a poet, you have a license to exaggerate and embellish with your language to convey your feelings toward your partner. If you looked rationally and objectively at your partner, you would have to think of the negatives that you find frustrating or difficult. That is why you can be less than rational while making emotional/psychological love to your partner. Complimenting each other reinforces a positive reciprocal feeling in the relationship. Couples need to continue to vow their love for each other poetically through complimentary responses. It is important for couples to take advantage of every opportunity to positively reinforce their relationship. There should be compliments and "I love you" every day. Every "fight" or negotiation of a difference should end with the use of endearing language and positive reinforcement of their feelings for each other. Couples who cannot engage in this process need to work on their relationship. If they cannot, their relationship is emotionally handicapped.

Women seem to be able to do this much easier than most men. So many men are taught that soft emotion is weakness and that real men are never weak. Although men are not called "sluts" or "whores," they *are* called "sissy," "pussy," "chicken," "chicken shit," "yellow," "yellow belly," "yellow-bellied coward," "coward," "weakling," and "candy ass." Any tears a boy may have around his peers will label him a "cry baby." Men are not supposed to ever be "needy" or show vulnerability or weakness. Posturing as strong and in control often covers up a man's softness and sensitivity. It also teaches him to repress any feelings that could be judged as weaknesses. Feelings of fear, insecurity, and anxiety are kept hidden for fear he will look weak and unmanly. Remember, men never ask for directions! To do so would be admitting a weakness. They must be logical and self-contained to appear in command. This male "condition" is part of the negative sexual script's definition of a man. It is part of the gender role stereotype for males—to be strong and in control.

REMOVING YOUR MASK

We all wear a social mask. There is what is referred to as the "public self" and the "private self." The public self is the mask we wear in public. We present ourselves as feeling good and doing well. We hide the more private feelings of not doing so well, not feeling so good. We are all taught how to conduct ourselves in public. We are polite, respectful, helpful, and generally a nice person who has no problems or worries. The public self has no financial, health, or personal problems. We are taught to put on the "happy face" in public and hide our true feelings from public view. When couples meet, they usually present the "public self" because they want to make a good impression. They want to be liked and loved. If the courtship isn't too long, the private self often will not be revealed in its entirety until a couple has locked into living together or marrying. Real emotional intimacy happens when the private selves meet.

Again, it seems that it is easier for most women to reveal their private self than it is for most men. So many men feel that what makes them "lovable" is the appearance of being strong, powerful, and in control. They falsely fear that if they show any weakness, they will not be loved by a woman. What so many men do not understand is that "hard feelings protect, but soft feelings connect." In emotional intimacy, it is important to let the soft emotion have expression. Expressing your sensitivity creates a feeling of closeness and connection.

When using endearing language with your partner, you are releasing the sensitive, poetic, and romantic dimension of yourself. You are sharing your sensitivity with your partner. Couples who learn to do this with each other will develop a very close love bond. The emotion or feeling that endearing language creates is soft, warm, and empathic. You are making psychological love to each other. At first, it may feel awkward and uncomfortable. But if you continue to express the language of love and endearment, you not only will get comfortable with the language but also will find that you really do feel the words you are saying. Redundancy is crucial. You cannot learn any new behavior without repetition. By repeating this process over and over, you not only establish a very positive pattern in your relationship but also establish emotional intimacy.

KEEPING MUSIC, POETRY, AND THEATER IN YOUR MARRIAGE

Imagine that a dictator took over our culture and made it against the law to have music. All forms of music were destroyed. Anyone caught listening to or playing music would be executed. Art and drama were also made against the law. Can you imagine what life would be like without art? Without music? Without theater? Music, art, and theater are what inspires our life spirit. They can lift us out of the monotony of the routine to transcendent levels of inspiration and peak experience. Music and art make us feel. Whether produced on film, performed live on stage, printed on a page, or recorded on a CD, music, art, and theater are the food of our life spirit—spiritual nourishment. Think how often you listen to music. Music is played not just on CDs or through streaming services and during concerts but also in the background for everything from movies to TV shows, to the news.

Romance is the music in any love relationship. When couples stop romancing each other, they have stopped the music, removed the art, and closed the theater in their relationship. Couples need to learn how to romance each other. They need to open their hearts to each other and express their love feelings. When you are celebrating your partner with compliments and love language, you are making music and poetry with your partner. Romancing is opening your heart to each other. Do you remember how you felt when you said your vows to each other? How you expressed your feelings for each other when you made the decision to live together? Remember the strong feelings of attraction you felt when you first started seeing each other? Romancing is keeping those feelings alive! Couples need to continue to play love music to each other.

There are numerous sources for learning how to do this. For males the best source is listening to your female partner. Ask her what romancing means to her and she will be glad to teach you. Yes, it's about flowers and cards. It's about love notes and being thoughtful and considerate. It's about repeatedly mentioning everything you appreciate and love about your partner. Another source that will model how to romance is movies, especially those "chick flicks" that most women love. Guys should start watching those films to learn about how important romance is to a relationship with a woman. Positive reinforcement, created by the process of romancing each other, puts the music, poetry, and theater in your relationship. This will not only strengthen and secure your relationship but will also markedly improve your sexual experience. Sex, Romance, Music, and Poetry are the four stars of a great relationship.

I would not recommend this process when you are upset with each other over something. Couples need to learn how to fight creatively so that they can resolve their differences. "Language of endearment" is what you express when you are getting along really well, after you have resolved a conflict and are feeling good about each other. It is a way of telling each other that you feel good that you are together. The focus should be on what your partner does right—what you love and appreciate about your partner, what you find satisfying in the relationship. It is all about exchanging positive messages with each other. Couples need to reinforce the positive qualities in their partners. Positive reinforcement—created by the process of romancing each other and using both the dating and endearment processes—will strengthen the relationship and secure your marriage.

INFIDELITY AND MONOGAMY

One day I am talking to a woman who tells me she has been having an affair with the man who lives across the street. The affair has been going on for twenty-five years and her husband doesn't know; the man's wife doesn't know either! I ask her, "How could you ever pull that off for twenty-five years?" She explains that her husband works during the day and she works night shift as a nurse. Her paramour works nights and his wife works days. Perfect! They never cross the street—never. Her lover has a very close, single male friend who lets them use his apartment during the day; that is where they meet. They have been exceptionally and extraordinarily discreet, to say the least! But the reason she is consulting with me is because her husband is retiring and will be home every day. She doesn't want to stop the affair, but she doesn't want a divorce either. She is stuck in the impasse of a decision she made twenty-five years ago.

Most marriages in America are monogamous. The National Health and Social Life Survey, considered to be a very respectable and legitimate piece of research, found that 25 percent of men and 15 percent of women surveyed admitted to having extramarital affairs. The Kinsey Institute published data indicating that 37 percent of males and 29 percent of females have been unfaithful at least once. Some studies estimate that 60 percent of married men and 40 percent of married women are unfaithful at some time during their marriage. While there may be a slight increase in these statistics, monogamy is still practiced by the majority, not only in marriages but in all relationships. There is of course the current concept of the "new monogamy," which reads like the old "open marriage" fad of the 1970s. If I sound a bit pessimistic about a couple who claim to love and be committed to each other but agree that it is OK to have sexual affairs with others when they want to, well, the truth is, I am. I am sure somewhere in this great big world there are couples who are living the new monogamy or the old open marriage and believe it works. I always wonder, though, just how long it will work and what kind of a relationship they really have.

If your relationship matures so that you truly feel the connection you have with your partner, it's far more difficult to transgress. That feeling of loving someone keeps us from doing a lot of things. Because we are not naturally monogamous, loving someone doesn't necessarily remove the sexual interest in mating with lots of other people. That desire for variety is how nature designed us. Comedian Chris Rock said, "A man's fidelity is as good as his opportunity." That could be true, but I would say, "A man's fidelity is as good as his relationship." Another way to frame this would be to say, "A man's fidelity is as good as his integrity." This also applies to women.

I have had a good number of couples see me over the past forty years who found that having affairs was fun in the beginning but became a miserable "deal-breaking disaster" to their relationship. I have also found that most couples don't get divorced because of an affair. While it is painful and agonizing, they work it out and most often look back on that event with a mixed feeling of "It was awful to go through, but we have a better relationship for having gone through it." Fortunately, people can and do learn and mature. When I counsel a couple who are dealing with this issue, I feel they need to work on their relationship in two different dimensions: They have to deal with all the hurt, pain, and distrust the affair almost always causes; and they have to regress in their relationship to evaluate what was going on between them prior to the beginning of the affair. If a couple is actively dating and relating (as previously discussed and described), the odds of an infidelity are just about nil. If a couple is making their relationship a priority, making sure they are having contact time daily, and continuing to enrich their sex life together, it is very doubtful there will be an infidelity.

Heterosexual men commit to a monogamous relationship with their wives not because they do not desire to have sex with other women, but rather because they have a strong sense of integrity. Most adult men and women have a sense of honesty and values that make them feel it is wrong to have an affair. They are aware that it would be very hurtful to their partner. They also know that it would be a violation and that they would feel guilty about what they had done. For many married men and women, having an affair is just wrong. They are committed to being monogamous, and they will not break that promise.

Tom and Jackie have been monogamous together during their forty-one years of marriage, and it appears that most married couples in America maintain monogamy. Infidelity is very hurtful and sometimes destructive to a marriage. It destroys the trust in the relationship. It is humiliating and undermines the self-esteem of the offended party. In many cases it puts an end to the marriage. For some people, it is an offense so hurtful that they cannot stay in the relationship.

Bill and Jane have been married eleven years. They had a child their third year of marriage and another child their fifth year of marriage. Before they had children, they had a very good sex life together. They remember having sex five times or more a week. With the birth of their first child, their sexual relationship started to change. Jane was tired from working and taking care of the baby. She felt exhausted almost every night. Sex just seemed like another chore she had to do before she could get to sleep. They started to have less sex. With the birth of their second child, things changed dramatically. Their sex life all but stopped completely. Then something else happened.

Bill felt that Jane was spending all her time caring for the children and not caring for him. He felt that Jane's time and her thoughts were all about the children. It seemed that all she could talk about was the children. She only became excited when the children did something cute or funny that she wanted to share. Bill came to the realization that Jane had emotionally divorced him and married their children. The children came first in everything. She spent all her spare time talking and playing with the children. All she wanted to talk about with Bill was the children. The only time he felt any approval from Jane was when he played with the children. He felt angry at Jane and started to withdraw; it seemed that Jane did not even care. Bill started feeling that all Jane wanted was the children and that was the only reason she married him. Whenever he tried to tell her what he was feeling, she got angry with him. She would go through a long list of the things she had to do, how tired she was, and how he was not helping enough. She would attack him with comments about how he did not appreciate her and all that she was doing.

Jane went to bed right after she put the children to bed, and Bill spent most evenings alone. He started staying up late watching pornography. He then got on a porn chat site. He started communicating with a woman who sounded interested in him. It was not too long before Bill discovered that the sexy woman he was talking with lived in his own town. He made a date with her, and they met one night after work for a drink. He told Jane he had to work late. The woman's name was Susan. She was very attracted to Bill, and he was very attracted to her. They started a sexual relationship. It was not too long before Jane noticed that Bill was acting strange. He was working late almost every night. On the weekends he often had to go back to the office. At home, he acted tired all the time. He did not talk much to her anymore. He did not have much sexual interest in her. In fact, when she asked him if he wanted to have sex, he said he was too tired.

Talking with some of her girlfriends, Jane mentioned how tired Bill was and how hard he was working. Her friends became very suspicious that Bill was having an affair and told Jane to check up on him. While

Bill was gone, she checked his e-mail and found the evidence confirming her girlfriends' suspicions.

Jane was shocked. She could not believe that Bill could do such a thing. The hurt cut through her like a knife. She felt a rush of anger. She felt she had to leave him, yet she knew she still loved him. She now felt a total distrust of him. She felt confusion because she loved him but hated him for what he had done. She wanted him to leave immediately; at the same time, she did not want him to go. She waited for Bill to come home. When he did, she had dozens of questions. "How long has this affair been going on?" "Do you love her?" "Have you had other affairs?" "Why did you do this?" "How could you do this to me?" "Did you tell her anything about me?" "Where does she live?" "How many times have you had sex with her?" "Where did you have sex with her?"

The questions kept coming. They were repetitive. Jane tried to make sense out of her confusion. She could not believe Bill would do this to her and his family. Bill did not know what to say. He felt guilty, sorry, apologetic, and ashamed. He kept telling Jane that he loved her and would do anything to keep their marriage. He said he was willing to get marriage counseling.

In counseling, Bill and Jane learned that they needed to work on a number of issues. They had to deal with all the feelings created by Bill's affair. Jane had to sort out all her feelings and decide whether she was going to divorce Bill or try to work things out. They also had to address the problems that existed in their relationship before Bill's affair.

DUALISM, DISTANCE, DISHONESTY, AND INFIDELITY

People involved in a clandestine affair are living two lives. One is with their marriage partner; the other is with their paramour. They must hide their lover from their partner. Time spent seeing their lover is time away from their partner, as well as their family life. Finding time to be with their paramour often involves lying and being dishonest. Thinking about and spending time with the person they are involved with puts more distance between them and their partner. This often makes the marriage more difficult. Over time, the capacity for duplicity erodes one's sense of integrity, which is perhaps the most insidious problem.

Most important, the third party becomes a distraction from confronting the issues in the marriage that led to the infidelity in the first place.

In some cases, an affair can be helpful to someone who is not in love with his or her partner. These people know they want out of the relationship but are not psychologically strong enough to leave. Often, having an affair gives them the confidence and support they need to leave a bad marriage or relationship.

Sometimes, getting involved with someone else can bring you to a deeper realization of the importance of your current partner. In such cases, the "cheating" partner stops the affair and turns the focus on his or her partner again. In the process of dealing with an infidelity, some couples fall back in love again. But in my experience working with couples dealing with infidelity, most suffer permanent damage that is difficult to repair.

INFIDELITY CAN DESTROY THE FEELING OF LOVE

Some couples cannot work out the damage done when one of them has become involved with someone else. I have known both men and women who, upon learning of their partner's affair, immediately contact an attorney and file for divorce. These people cannot forgive or forget the hurt the affair caused them to feel. The relationship has been killed. I have observed couples that spend two years in marriage counseling, trying to heal the hurt, anger, and distrust an affair creates. At the end of the counseling, the offended party still files for divorce. Some aggrieved people feel they cannot heal from the hurt if they stay in the marriage.

I have known couples that stay together after an infidelity, but the feeling of "being in love" is gone. The trust and respect the offended party once had for the offending spouse has been scuttled. They often stay together for the children. Sometimes they cannot afford a divorce, or their religious beliefs do not permit it. They stay together, but their relationship is never the same; the level of damage is too severe to ever restore the feeling of love. For some couples the hurt never leaves, and the lost love and trust never returns.

THE PROCESS OF HEALING FROM AN INFIDELITY

How do couples heal from an infidelity? The healing involves a process that can help repair the damage done—if a couple can follow it. A couple must deal with both the feelings they had between them before the start of the affair and the feelings they now have since the discovery of the affair. It is doubtful that a couple with a close emotional connection can allow a third party to come between them. The issues they had before the start of an affair disconnected them. Had they addressed those issues, there may not have been an infidelity. The unaddressed problems often contribute to the reason for the affair. Once the affair is discovered, they need to address this crisis in their relationship.

Because of the complexity of having to work out issues on two different levels—before the affair and after the affair—it is often helpful for a couple to seek help from a competent marriage counselor. Discussing the "before and after" feelings and issues is an important part of the healing process. The offended party often feels that things were "good" between them when the affair started. In some cases, the offended party was not even aware of the problems or knew there were issues but did not feel they were that serious. Often the offending party has not been direct or honest with his or her spouse about dissatisfaction in the marriage. In some cases, both had been in denial of the problems existing between them.

What I have found important to the healing process is the need for the offended partner to be able to express his or her hurt, anger, and distrust to the spouse over and over again. This process is redundant. The hurt partner needs to repetitively ask the same questions, and repetitively express the same feelings he or she has about the affair. If the offending spouse can understand the need for repetitious expression over weeks and months of the pain he or she has caused, the relationship often starts to improve. This working-out process is really a form of desensitization. Repetitive discussion of the feelings can "wear them out" so they become less and less a topic of discussion.

What is most difficult in this process is the reaction of the partner who had the affair. Because the offender feels the affair has been discussed several times, he or she feels the issue should be resolved. He or she has made an apology, and the details of the event have been made transparent. A promise of commitment and love has been assured, so why should a couple keep talking about it? People need to understand that the healing process is redundant so that feelings can be exhausted, worked out, and worn out. This requires patience, understanding, and empathy on the part of the offending partner. Even though all the questions have been answered multiple times, this repeated verbosity helps in the healing. The offender can usually get past the affair with a confession, an apology, and a sworn commitment to never do it again, but the offended party must heal a broken heart and a crushed soul! The offended party has experienced a serious breach in feeling trust in his or her partner. Healing is always more difficult for the offended than the offender.

INFIDELITY CAN BE WORKED OUT AND THE RELATIONSHIP IMPROVED

Many couples can resolve the suffering and distrust created by an affair. The affair opens honest communication at a level they had never known before. Going through the process of healing from the affair improves their relationship and gives them a more intimate connection. They begin to feel closer than they were before the affair happened. Years later, these couples feel that although the affair was awful, it was the best thing that ever happened to their relationship. They not only learned a lot, but their relationship improved because of that experience. They learned to communicate more honestly and more directly. They learned to listen to each other and to make time to keep in contact.

Couples need to learn to live in the present and not in the past. The focus should be on the "here and now," not on what happened years ago. If they can create meaning and pleasure in the here and now, they will feel a connection that transcends some painful event in the past.

I have also observed that when a married person no longer loves his or her spouse and wants a divorce, having an affair can be very helpful, especially when he or she does not have the psychological strength to leave. An affair can give people the support and confidence to leave a marriage that is no longer right for them.

THE INFIDELITY PREVENTION FORMULA

There is a formula for the prevention of infidelity. A couple that makes a joint effort to follow this formula will have almost 100 percent protection against either partner getting involved with a third party. Consider how Tom and Jackie managed to be together forty-one years without infidelity. When you compare Tom and Jackie's marriage to Bill and Jane's, you can see major differences between them. Tom and Jackie follow the infidelity prevention formula; Bill and Jane do not. Here is a review of what Tom and Jackie do that keeps fidelity in their relationship.

1. They allow and respect each other's independence and personal freedom. They give each other space to do what each likes to do. They do not get in each other's way. They support each other's private interests. There is a wide margin of freedom in the relationship for them to do what they like to do without their partner. They do not need to do everything together. They both support the fact that they have an independent private life within their marriage.

2. No one in the relationship has dominant control of the other. There is no "boss" in this marriage. They work at maintaining a peer relationship. Each respects the other's feelings. When they disagree, they negotiate through the difference together, with no one dictating the solution. All solutions must be agreeable to both partners.

3. They follow the rules of good communication. They both actively listen to each other. When one of them is talking, the other does not interrupt. They wait their turn to express what they are feeling. All feelings and points of view are respected and considered. Differences are negotiated to a place where both can agree. They do not attack each other's self-esteem by labeling and name-calling. They understand that in a disagreement, no one's perspective is right or wrong. They see the issue differently, and they negotiate and compromise to reach an agreement that satisfies them both.

4. They are very open about their sexuality. They have rid themselves of sexual fears, guilt, shame, and embarrassment. They not only have developed an openness in talking about sex but are able to share with each other their most personal and private sexual feelings. They have rid themselves of most of their inhibitions. They have an understanding that sex can be a lighthearted activity that is mostly erotic fun, or it can be a serious and emotionally intense, intimate event. Both are comfortable having sex with themselves. Masturbation is an accepted and expected ongoing practice for them both. Pornography is also accepted as a visual aphrodisiac and is not considered "threatening" or something that must be viewed in private. They both understand male sexuality and the high levels of sexual tension that males have to manage. They maintain an active sex life with each other and can talk openly and freely about any sexual needs or feelings either of them may have." Sex alone is not enough glue to keep a couple together, but sexual conflict can inspire infidelity and divorce.

5. They use the "language of endearment" in their communication. They both flood their communication to each other with compliments and many "I love you" messages. They understand how important positive reinforcement is to their relationship. They both pay attention for opportunities to give each other support, compliments, help, and love. They have learned to speak affectionately to each other. In addition, they give each other a lot of nonsexual physical touch. When sitting on the sofa while watching television, one of them will give a foot rub to the other. At night when they get in bed, one of them will massage the other's shoulders or back. They always hug and kiss goodbye and greet each other with a hug. Sometimes when they are passing in the living room or down a hallway, they will reach out and touch. It is a common practice for either of them to look the other straight in the face, smile, and say, "I love you." They look for ways to give each other validation.

6. Tom and Jackie are very aware of their attractions to other people. They know the idea that there is just one man for each woman and one woman for each man is complete nonsense. They believe there are thousands of compatible partners for everyone. They both know they are occasionally going to meet one of those "also compatible" partners. When they do, they will feel the rapport, the affinity, and the physical attraction. While they recognize that they would like to get involved with this "attractive" person, upon this recognition, they set the boundary immediately. Neither of them ever flirts because they know that flirting suggests that you are available if the other party is willing. They also do not confide personal feelings to someone else that should only belong to their relationship. They never tell this "attractive" person anything they have not shared with each other. Lastly, Tom and Jackie talk and laugh about other people they find attractive. This is not a threatening conversation, because they always validate what they love about each other and about being together.

7. Tom and Jackie have an agreement about feeling sexual. They agree that they can be turned on by other people or by fantasies of sex with others, be that pictures, thoughts, or a real person. They have made a commitment: They are to fulfill all sexual feelings by having sex with themselves or with each other. They are very clear about their agreement to be sexually exclusive, which for them means absolutely no sexual contact with anyone else, but that does not apply to what and how they become turned on in fantasy.

Couples who work on these seven areas in their marriages will develop a deeper and stronger bond against infidelity. However, this formula for the prevention of infidelity does not work with all couples. There are some individuals, both male and female, whose personalities are borderline, sociopathic, or narcissistic. These psychological conditions keep them from maintaining boundaries. They are often so self-centered and needy that they cannot maintain fidelity or integrity. Marriage counseling, even psychotherapy, will rarely help them. These individuals have a form of mental illness that is usually therapy proof. For these couples, marriage is doomed to chronic misery or divorce.

A couple can go through a wedding ceremony and sign a marriage license, but that does not make them married. They are married on paper but often have not wed each other emotionally. It is only when a couple feels a deep emotional, psychological, spiritual, and physical connection that they are truly married. It is not easy to stray in a marriage when you are not really married. When the emotional commitment has not been established, only vocalized, the relationship is vulnerable to a third-party involvement.

When we make the decision to marry someone, we are putting limits on our life. Actually, if you consider it, all decisions rule out other choices and limit your life. If I decide to head south, I have ruled out going north, east, or west. When I marry and agree to be sexually exclusive with my partner, I am ruling out having sex with anyone else. I am putting limits on my sexual experiences. I will be having sex with this one person for the rest of my life.

But also consider what you gain. No other relationship provides the opportunity to learn more about oneself than marriage does; you become known by your partner like no other person can know you, which includes both the wonderful parts of your personality as well as your dark side. You will have constant support throughout your lifetime. You will have a helpmate to make your life easier. You will never really be alone. You will have someone with whom to do things with anytime of the day or night. You will have someone with whom to share the enormity of life. You will have a person who gives you love and receives yours. You will have a continued opportunity for sexual satisfaction. You will build a shared history that provides great comfort in your aging years. You will have someone for whom you never have to put on that "social mask" to have acceptance. When your health is giving you problems, you will have a partner who gives a damn about you and will be there for you. If you and your partner want to have children and create a family, that is a unique experience that can be far more fulfilling than getting laid two thousand times.

The reality of our lives involves far more than just having sex. We need confidence, meaning, acceptance, love, support, understanding, and someone to help share the struggle of life. We need medical care and a career that can support us. Most of all we need social connection. Birds fly in a flock, cattle are in a herd, fish swim in schools, and humans have always had connection to a tribe. Being in a relationship with someone is important to most people. Marriage has the potential to connect us to a partner, as well as a social culture, which seems very important to mental health and good psychological adjustment in life. I recognize that marriage is not for everyone, nor should everyone have children. Living together in a committed relationship can also provide many of these benefits.

For most people, marriage can fulfill a deep primary need that is basic to existence. Early in the social development of human life, male and female coupled up and created a family. Marriage is a social recognition of that coupling within a culture.

9

CONCLUSION

Breaking Free of the Negative Sexual Script and Living More Erotically

According to the Associated Press, a nineteen-year-old woman in Wellington, New Zealand, offered to sell her virginity to the highest bidder on her website.[1] She was raising money to pay her college tuition. More than thirty thousand people viewed her ad. Twelve hundred men made bids for her virginity, and she accepted an offer of more than thirty-two thousand dollars. How could she do this? Prostitution is legal in New Zealand. Advertising sexual services in ads and online is also legal.

In the Netherlands, comprehensive sex education is provided to young people by their parents, who believe that when a child becomes old enough to have sex, he or she probably will. They do not teach abstinence in their homes or their schools. What they do teach is responsibility. Birth control is provided by the government to teenagers, and abortion is free. It is no wonder that the Netherlands has the lowest teen birth rate and the lowest abortion rate among developed nations![2]

Sweden begins teaching preschool children where babies come from, how they are made, and how you can keep from making a baby. They have comprehensive sex education in their schools and provide birth control to teenagers. Sweden has the second lowest teenage pregnancy rate among developed nations. Abortion is also free and, compared to America, Sweden's abortion rate is minuscule.[3]

America has the highest teen pregnancy rate among all developed nations. Our sexual legacy teaches abstinence until marriage.[4] Our sexual script is to suppress and censure sexual interest by our young people. There is still a strong movement in American culture to censor comprehensive sex education and to deny birth control to young women as well as all forms of abortion, including the "morning-after" pill.

In Sweden and Denmark, erotic films are shown early in the evening during prime time, but violent American movies are shown late at night, when the kids are in bed. In most of Europe, people swim in public in the nude and women can sun topless on the beaches. That is against the law in most of America. In the Scandinavian countries, families enjoy being nude in their saunas together, and that may include not just Mom and Dad and the children but also Grandma and Grandpa. Unlike Americans, they are very relaxed about nudity. In America, a family swimming nude together would be considered "perverted," and the adults could be arrested for lewd conduct.

MANGAIA

This brings us to one of the most sexual places known in the world: the island of Mangaia. This very small (only twenty miles long and about five miles wide) island in the Polynesian chain some 165 miles north of New Zealand is closed to the outside world. Covered in mango, breadfruit, and coconut trees, the island has no hotels or restaurants and no port. My partner in marriage, Dr. Joan Henderson, and I went to Mangaia in 1994. We had to get permission to visit from one of the fewer than fifteen hundred people who live on the island. We also had to get one of the families who live on the island to accept us as guests. To get to the island, you travel from Los Angeles, to Hawaii, to Tahiti, and then to Rarotonga, where you get on a small airplane that flies you to the beach landing strip (no airport) on Mangaia. Walking is your only transportation; there are no cars, and that plane you came in on won't be back for a week.

I learned about Mangaia's very permissive and open sexual practices from an anthropological study done by Donald S. Marshall.[5] The ethos of the island is about both sexual pleasure and procreation. Sex education on this island is more than comprehensive; it is experiential! When a Mangaian boy reaches about the age fifteen, he is educated about sex. He is instructed in the importance of making certain his female partner has at least three orgasms before he climaxes. He is told about the importance of the woman's clitoris and how to suck a woman's breast to stimulate her and to get her very "wet" before entering. He is taught other techniques to stimulate her erogenous zones. He is then taken by an older female, often widowed, who has sex with him and "checks him out," showing him different positions and making certain he is doing everything correctly.[6]

Teenage girls on the island are taught the importance of orgasm and are instructed on how to use "hip motion" to increase pleasure. They are taught about the importance of the clitoris, getting wet, and being active in seeking pleasure. Parents want their daughters to have sex with many partners, and an eighteen-year-old male on Mangaia will average three orgasms every day with a partner.[7] All women on Mangaia have multiple orgasms. When I asked some of the women about anyone not having an orgasm, they laughed and acted astounded at the very thought—they could not even imagine having sex without an orgasm.

Think for a minute. What was your sexual education like? Did anyone give you clear, honest, and direct information that gave you confidence and competence in being sexual? Do you think America has a negative sexual script?

If you really believe that America's sexual beliefs and teachings positively affirm our sexuality, you are suffering from massive denial, ignorance, or both! No matter what party is running our government, Democrats or Republicans, they fund millions of dollars for the teaching of abstinence in our schools. Recently states have been given the option of teaching both abstinence and comprehensive sex education; they can get funding for both. But the majority of schools in America still teach abstinence only. The abstinence until marriage script is still the sexual script of the American culture, and some states reject anything other than abstinence being taught in their high schools.[8]

Other cultures do not have sexual issues in their political elections. In America, a candidate can rise or fall simply on his or her spoken beliefs about birth control, abstinence, abortion, or the morning-after pill. I won't even get into the subject of gay rights and gay marriage. While this culture gives us a lot of sexual teasing that can be arousing, it doesn't provide important information about our sexuality. It does provide a lot of shame and guilt. We are taught to be fearful not just about being sexual but also about asking questions and seeking accurate, honest, information. We have a difficult time talking about the subject. The fact that families can't talk about sex and avoid the subject communicates that sex is shameful and naughty. Children's questions about sex are met with silence and awkwardness from their parents. Young people cannot get accurate information.

One of countless examples of sexual censorship and suppression happened in a high school in Meridian, Idaho, when a nurse was invited to teach a group of high school seniors about HIV prevention and other STDs.[9] This was a voluntary group of seniors, not a required class. As one part of the lecture, she talked about condoms. Many young people don't know there is a way to put condoms on and take them off to prevent a spill or leak that could risk pregnancy. If you put them on wrong, you can cause a break; if you take them off wrong, you can cause a leak. The nurse used a banana to illustrate the correct way to use a condom. When word got out about this, parents were outraged. The teacher was suspended and severely rebuked. The nurse was banned from ever speaking again on that campus. A large volume of angry parents wrote condemning letters to the editor of the local newspaper, voicing their moral indignation.

After teaching Human Sexuality to thousands of students over a twenty-five-year period at Boise State University, I have witnessed the difficulty young people who are just becoming sexual have with the whole issue. Working with thousands of couples in my private marriage counseling practice over forty years has also given me information and insight into the struggle couples have with sex. The students I taught ranged from eighteen to thirty years old. The couples I work with in my private practice range in age from around thirty-five to fifty-five years old. What amazed me was that there was not a whole lot of difference between these two groups when it came to the subject of sex. I witnessed massive ignorance from very intelligent people, both young and old. I still find surprising fear and inhibition. It seems that most women of any age struggle with being able to have orgasms and also with feeling desire for sex. Certainly there are exceptions, but I am talking generally about averages. Whether it was in a college classroom or a marriage counseling session, I discovered that too many women reject masturbation and feel guilt and shame even talking about the subject.

I am not just talking about thirty or forty years ago. In 2014 a lecture and discussion in a college Human Sexuality class continued to validate the shame, guilt, inhibition, and embarrassment most women feel in discussing sex, especially masturbation. All research on masturbation finds a low percentage of women who masturbate.[10] Males generally are sexually frustrated and have anxiety about their sexual adequacies and performance, but research shows they are much more comfortable with masturbation and sex talk.

There appears to be some change and improvement in the younger generation. A percentage of young teens and college-age people are more open about sex and are having more sex, but that is still a minority of our population. I have had these students in class, and sex is still problematic for them. Sixty to 70 percent of people in America have their first intercourse by age sixteen, and almost 90 percent have had their first intercourse by age twenty. If sex education, especially that promoting abstinence only, is so good in America, why do we have the highest teen pregnancy rate among all developed countries in the West?

Books are still being banned for seniors in high schools all over the United States. In 2014 the trustees at the Meridian School District in Meridian, Idaho, banned the National Book Award–winning novel *The Absolutely True Diary of a Part-Time Indian* by Sherman Alexie from the school's library and senior reading list after parents complained about the book's mention of masturbation and use of profanity.[11] The book won the National Book Award for Young People's Literature in 2007, and the National Coalition against Censorship stated in a letter to the school board: "The novel addresses vital issues such as the struggles of young adulthood, the search for personal identity, bullying and poverty." The letter continued, saying that the book "is ultimately an uplifting story of triumph by a boy with few advantages."

Examples of book banning and/or controversy regarding comprehensive sex instruction in American schools in Alabama, Delaware, Maryland, Kentucky, Colorado, Arizona, Missouri, Arkansas, Kansas, Tennessee, South Carolina, Pennsylvania, Florida, Texas, and Illinois can be found in the Sexuality Controversy Database in the records of Sexuality Information and Education Council of the United States (SIECUS).[12] The good news is that the database is showing a trend toward approval of comprehensive sex education and a move away from abstinence-only education. There is also some important progress toward acceptance of gay marriage in thirty-seven states, and in 2015 the Supreme Court of the United States ruled that marriage equality was a right nationwide. However, there is an increase in controversy regarding LGBTQ—lesbian, gay, bisexual, transgender, questioning—gender identity issues. Most of the controversy is over the discussion of these issues in schools. There is even more controversy over whether schools should teach about contraception and allow speakers from organizations such as Planned Parenthood. Many Americans view Planned Parenthood as an organization that "pushes" kids to be sexually active and to get abortions when, in fact, it includes abstinence in its comprehensive sex model. The real problem some Americans have with Planned Parenthood is that the organization provides honest, accurate, comprehensive sex education. Planned Parenthood receives the same hostility that such sexual educators as Hugh Heffner, Alfred Kinsey, Wardell Pomeroy, and Masters and Johnson received for promoting sex education. The federal government still funds abstinence-only education in schools, even though it has been proven a failure in preventing the spread of sexually transmitted disease and teen pregnancy.[13]

According to *Webster's Dictionary*, the word "hoodwinked" means to deceive, delude, dupe, mislead, bamboozle, or snow. Advocates of the negative sexual script have hoodwinked the American people. A large segment of our population has been taught to feel guilt, shame, and fear about our natural sexuality. The erotophobes have deluded parents into being afraid to teach sex to their children. There are certainly plenty of exceptions, but too many parents have been duped into thinking it is better not to provide their children with positive sexual information. They wrongly believe that ignorance is better.

Most children in other industrialized countries receive comprehensive sex education. Instead of being taught abstinence from sex until marriage, they are taught responsible sexuality. Other industrialized countries also provide information on contraception and make contraceptives readily available to teenagers. In America, teenagers must buy their own contraception, which many of them can't afford. Since we have solid research that close to 60 percent of Americans will have their first intercourse by age sixteen and that 90 percent will have their first intercourse by age twenty,[14] would it not make more sense to take the money we spend on teaching abstinence and provide information on and access to birth control, as so many other countries are doing? We do not, and we have the highest teen birth rate among all industrialized countries. We have too many fourteen- , fifteen- , and sixteen-year-old children having children because of our negative sexual script. Even more damaging, the purveyors of the negative sexual script have so demonized the fine work done by Planned Parenthood that people are afraid to use its services.

Abundant research from our finest universities confirms that first-century Christian teachings on sexuality do not work in the twenty-first century. This scripting from the first century and the Middle Ages has had a negative effect on our sexuality. It has contributed to the inhibition, guilt, and fear people have about allowing erotica into their lives. It is also responsible for the sexual frustration so many couples have in their marriage.

When I asked my students what they thought was America's official sexual script, they talked about how sexy America is and all the sexual freedom there is in this culture. However, when I tested them on sexual anatomy, only a few nursing students passed. When I asked how they felt about masturbation, most of the responses were negative—and most of that negative response was from the women.

Young people may feel they have sexual freedom, but many of them are dealing with sexual frustration and inhibitions. The males are struggling with sexual frustration and performance anxiety; the females are struggling with difficulty having orgasms and inhibitions created by the fear of being a slut or a whore.

I hear men complain about how much their partners reject them when they approach them for sex. I hear complaints from female partners about how mechanical their sex life feels. I hear clients confess that they feel little sexual desire for their partner. Many males cannot share erotica with their female partner, so they hide the fact that they like viewing it. I keep hearing from women who feel they should never think outside the box when it comes to sexuality and hardly think about the subject at all. What has happened to their erotic dimension? Where is their lust? Have they disconnected from their natural mating urge?

When my students first come to class, they think they know everything about sex. They are in denial. As the "professor of sex," I would be the first to tell you that I do not know everything about sex. Students are amazed when I tell them that the withdrawal method of birth control rarely works and actually is very risky. Why? Because of the Cowper's gland—a little gland in the male that secretes a cleaning fluid when his penis becomes erect. The fluid travels down the urethra and neutralizes any urinary acids, cleaning and preparing the urinary canal for the sperm. This clear or slightly white fluid often carries live sperm. Even though the male has not ejaculated, the female can still get pregnant from the fluid produced by the Cowper's gland. How many teenage girls become pregnant because they and their partner do not have this information? Important information like this is being ignored in almost all sexuality classes in American high schools. We are not allowed, we are afraid, or we just do not know how to properly teach young people how to have sex, how to protect themselves from sexually transmitted infections, and how to prevent pregnancy.

When our young people marry or start to live with a partner, they bring their unresolved sexual issues into their relationship. These issues are often exacerbated by the responsibilities of everyday reality. People become stuck in "everyday reality"—working on career goals; establishing and maintaining a house or other place to live; buying furnishings, a better car, and all the little extras that put them in debt and increase the stress in their life. Starting a family makes even more demands on their time and energy. They make their "to-do list," but sex is usually not on it. Fatigue pushes sexual desire into the background. Because the male brain is so visual and the sexual mating urge is so strong in most males, they don't lose their focus on sexual desire, as so many women do. But they do lose their focus on the interpersonal issues of their relationship. Generally speaking, males think more about wanting sex with their partner than they do about romancing, relating, listening, and validating the woman they say they love.

Women in relationships often begin to feel less desire for sex. It is not that they don't want to have sex; it's just that they are too busy or too tired most of the time to connect with their erotic dimension. Often women are upset with what is going on interpersonally with their partner, and that can block their connection to their sexual desire. The result is that the male is turned on and his female partner is not in the mood. There are certainly couples where this is just the reverse. Many women feel sexually frustrated with their husbands, and it is the male who is not in the mood; but that is more the exception than the rule.

I have found that countless couples are having sexual difficulty in their relationship. Although America is one of the most sexualized countries in the world, sex is still one of the primary problems for young people as well as many older couples. We see sexual advertising images in almost every magazine. We have sex scenes in almost all R-rated movies, and television is saturated with sexual advertising, including comedians talking explicitly about sex and sitcoms with sex scenes. We also have unlimited access to pornography on cable and satellite television, our smartphones, and our computers.

While it seems that our culture is sexually free and open, how is it that so many couples struggle with sexual problems? Men struggle with performance issues such as getting and keeping an erection; women struggle with their lack of sexual desire and difficulty achieving an orgasm. Couples are inhibited and uncomfortable with erotica and deep erotic states. They are uncomfortable with erotic language. Many American women view good erotica as dirty. Males are spending more time watching porn and having sex with themselves, and more and more women have lost desire for sex.

When a couple can talk candidly about sex and not be ashamed or embarrassed, they are off to a good start. If they can joke about sex, share sexual innuendos, and use double entendres, they are demonstrating a relaxed sexual spirit that opens the gate to erotic freedom and expression. This is not easy for American couples, because the negative sexual conditioning of our culture makes them afraid that they might say something wrong or inappropriate. For countless couples, just using erotic language like "cock" or "cunt" or "fuck" is wrong. Furthermore, couples are afraid to share sexual fantasies for fear their partner might think them "kinky" or perverted. They are afraid to say or do something that might offend their partner.

Masters and Johnson studied several hundred couples regarding what they fantasize about while having sex with their partner.[15] More than 70 percent said they often fantasized that they were having sex with a complete stranger—someone they did not know and had never met. There is a risk in admitting this to your partner, because the negative sexual script teaches that you should only have desire for your partner.

One couple shared with me an experience they had while staying at a resort on a beach in Mexico. They had dinner at a restaurant on the beach. It was a beautiful romantic setting, with the sound of the ocean and a light warm breeze in the air. They ordered margaritas and an appetizer before dinner. While enjoying their appetizer and margaritas, they started talking about every sexual experience each had before they met each other, twenty-seven years ago. They started with very first erotic experience they could remember. Before they could finish their appetizer, they became so sexually aroused that they had to tell the waiter to hold their table. They rushed back to their condo and had passionate hot sex before returning to finish their dinner. Sharing their past sexual experiences was an ultimate turn-on. They obviously were a secure couple who were not at all threatened by their partner's past lovers.

When couples can tell each other what they like and don't like, what turns them on, and what fantasies excite them, when they use erotic language that stimulates arousal and are willing to be experimental with their partner, they will be creating a deeper erotic relationship. If Jane tells her male partner, "I'd like you to park your car in my garage," and he answers, "Cock-a-doodle-do," could that communication actually be a part of foreplay? If she says, "Just looking at you makes me wet," and he replies, "Just looking at you makes my cock throb," would this communication begin to move them into a more erotic state?

The focus of many porn movies is on sexual stimulation and increasing desire and passion. The woman wants it as much as the man. Together, the man and woman do everything to give pleasure and to stimulate each other to orgasm. The male is giving pleasure to the female, and the female is giving pleasure to the male. They both get into a deep erotic state where each becomes focused on pleasure. There is no sexual frustration in erotic movies. There is no guilt, no shame, no inhibition, and no sexual restriction. Both the male and the female know exactly what to do to achieve maximum pleasure with each other. The male says, "Suck my dick," and the woman sucks his dick. In so many American marriages, the husband knows there is no point in even asking. The female says, "Eat my cunt," and the male licks her clitoris. In too many American marriages, the wife knows her husband does not like to go down on her. Too often the wife does not want oral stimulation, even if her husband wants to give her that pleasure. Why would a female not enjoy a soft, wet, warm tongue stroking her clitoris? Could it be because Saint Aquinas said it was sinful? Could it be because it is embarrassing to show so much vulnerability? Could it be that she is just focused on servicing her husband and not herself? Or is it that she just does not feel comfortable getting in a deep erotic state where she is completely surrendered to her own lust?

So many women have been socially conditioned by the negative sexual script that to really let themselves get "hot" and surrender to pleasure makes them feel that they are acting like a whore or a slut. That conditioning can make it more difficult a woman to reach orgasm. A thought: Could her inhibitions and "non-erotic rules" about sex inspire her husband to view porn to achieve sexual satisfaction?

I have heard women talk very negatively about pornography: "It isn't love; it's lust." "That male is using that female." "That woman is a whore, and I am not." "The female has been manipulated by males to do what she is doing. Real-life women and real-life sex are not that way."

Is it true that real-life couples are not able to respond sexually like the couple in a porn movie? The fact is, there are a few women and couples whose sex experience together is just like those couples in porn movies. Many erotic movies are actually made by amateur couples who are married to each other. Other, less-exhibitionist couples find that erotic movies have taught them how to have deep erotic sexual experience together and have thus been liberated from the negative sexual script. They enjoy very passionate, total-response lovemaking. I certainly recognize that most porn movies are made by actors, who are "acting" as the director directs them. But think of the sexual freedom one must have to make a porn movie!

I am amazed at the sexual ignorance so many men have about women and so many women have about men. Sexuality is at the epicenter of our biology. Our sexuality is a part of our nature. It is natural. It was with us when we walked on all fours as it is with us now. It should be easy, and it should be fun. It most certainly should be pleasurable.

Have the advocates of the negative sexual script achieved their goal of repressing, inhibiting, and restricting sexual enjoyment? Are we so embarrassed about our sexuality that we cannot talk about it openly with the person we love and live with—the person we sleep next to, eat with, and share everything with; the person we have built a life with? Too many couples cannot talk about their sexual feelings or needs with the person to whom they have committed to be sexually exclusive.

When it comes to the subject of sex, too many of us have guilt, shame, fear of masturbation; discomfort with oral stimulation, the rear-entry position, and the use of vibrators or sexual toys; talking about sex, viewing it, reading about it, and teaching it.

These are all problematic issues in our culture. We have been deceived; we have been deluded, tricked, bamboozled, hyped, snowed. We have been hoodwinked! We have been hoodwinked by the negative sexual script invented by a group of individuals, authorities, and institutions. They have invented this script because of their guilt, fear, and shame. They have for centuries projected their unnatural, fearful, and abnormal negative fears of sex. They have written a false script they want us all to use as the sexual standard. They are the erotophobes who fear their natural sexuality. While other Western nations seem to have evolved beyond these corrupted sexual views, America is still listening to and believing them. It is as though we are voting against ourselves.

GETTING A GRIP ON SEX

As a person ages, sexual desire and performance ability begins to diminish. For males, it can become more difficult to achieve and maintain firm erections and to release sexual tension through orgasm. For females, it can become more difficult to lubricate and reach an orgasm. Even more troubling is the loss of desire for sex.

As we grow older, our lives become more complex and busy. Work responsibilities take up more of our time and thought as we try to establish an economic foundation for our lives. If you add children to your life so that family responsibilities take over where work or professional duties leave off, sex is no longer in the foreground of your thoughts.

One of the most critical aging factors impacting our sexuality is our physical health. Sex involves physical activity that is not congruent with poor health. Continuing to exercise and keep in good physical condition is paramount. Hormone changes can also have a pronounced effect on sexual interest and functioning.

While it is true that elderly people can continue to have meaningful and enjoyable sex, it is also true that a good many lose the ability and interest to continue to be sexual. One national survey of men and women over the age of sixty found the following:[16]

- 71 percent of men and 51 percent of women are sexually active in their sixties.
- 57 percent of men and 30 percent of women are sexually active in their seventies.
- 25 percent of men and 20 percent of women are sexually active in their eighties.
- There is a continual decline in sexual interest and activity as we age.

Although there are many exceptions, most females have difficulty with maintaining their desire for sex, especially as they age. Most women also have difficulty with masturbation, pornography, and anything that is very explicit about sex. It is any wonder that sales of Viagra, Levitra, and Cialis are breaking records?

So now we come to the real point: We all need to get a *grip* on sex! By "grip," I mean we need to not let our sexuality *slip* away from us. Masters and Johnson taught that when it comes to sex, you need to *use it or lose it*!

Getting a grip on your sexuality means making your sexuality as important in your life as eating, drinking, and sleeping. Sex should be integrated into our daily routines. Instead of waiting for that moment to come upon us when we feel like having sex, we need to create that moment by thinking, reading, viewing, or discussing sex.

I know a sixty-eight-year-old woman who is still having multiple orgasms and responding to sexual stimulation like much younger people do. She has always kept her sexuality in the foreground of her life. She masturbates to orgasm almost daily and reads romance novels that are explicitly candid. She never avoids talking or joking about anything sexual. She enjoys some sexual thinking almost every day.

Maintaining sexual stimulation every day is to sexuality as eating food is to physical health. I know another woman, vice president of a large corporation, who is struggling to keep from losing her sexual desire because she is "too busy and tired" for sex. She put some porn on her iPhone that she can conveniently view during "breaks" in her busy day and said it improved her sex life with her husband considerably.

With all the responsibilities she has, it was easy for her to get stuck in everyday reality and ignore erotic reality.

One last important point: Masters and Johnson found that people who were very sexually active in their youth, who enjoyed having a lot of sex, continued to stay sexually active into old age.[17] So work out your hang-ups; enjoy your sexuality to the fullest, and you probably won't "lose it" when you reach old age.

REMEMBER: USE IT OR LOSE IT!

Increasing sexual desire and having a more erotic relationship are issues for a growing number of couples, especially in marriage and long-term relationships. Males are visual and hypersensitive when it comes to sexuality. While there are women who are no different in their sexual awareness and desire, they are in the minority in our society. For most women, sexual desire is not as easy to achieve as it is for males. Here is an important clue to this issue: Both the male and female brain will respond to anything sexual. When stimulated, a woman becomes "wet" in the same amount of time it takes a man to get an erection. If you focus on anything related to sex, the brain will turn on the desire! If you don't think about sex, read about sex, talk about sex, or look at sex, you most likely will have little desire for it.

Making your marriage more erotic is a process of rejecting the negative sexual script and becoming liberated from the conventional assumptions you have been taught about sexuality. By allowing erotic language and lustful expression into their relationship, a couple will not only experience more pleasure and sexual freedom together but will also feel more connected and bonded.

ALL PLAY AND NO WORK

Sex should be all play and no work. The "play" I am talking about in regard to sex is most widely known as foreplay. Foreplay is just that— the sexual play that takes place before sexual intercourse begins. Foreplay is the most important part of having sex. I am going to say it again: Foreplay is the most important part of having sex. Too many couples put the cart before the horse and begin too soon. This often results in mediocre sex, mechanical sex, or, worse yet, dysfunctional sex. For males the dysfunction is most often losing his erection after he begins to stroke and/or not being able to release and have an orgasm. For females the most common dysfunction is not being able to achieve orgasm.

Viagra, Levitra, and Cialis can help a man "get it up," but that is not a substitute for foreplay. A woman can "open the gate," but that alone is not enough to get her to maximum pleasure. Foreplay is itself a form of erotic pleasure. It is all about pleasuring your partner into a deep erotic state before intercourse begins. When a couple lays a deep erotic foundation to their lovemaking before intercourse, sex becomes all play and no work.

Your psychological attitude is most important. You need to be psychologically focused on sensation. Everything you think about should be erotic. Sexual fantasy is helpful, but more important is focusing on the pleasure you are receiving from the stimulation of your erogenous zones. Anything spoken should be erotic. This means getting everyday reality like your to-do list out of your head and concentrating on everything and anything erotic. If you are thinking about what you have to do tomorrow—or if while making out, you realize the bedroom needs painting—you are not in a proper psychological mind-set for making love. Focusing on the pleasurable sensations your partner is stimulating in you, and stimulating pleasurable sensation in your partner, is the foreplay that needs to take place before intercourse begins.

Foreplay is to sex as strings are to a guitar, as a foundation is to a house, as yeast is to baking bread, as wheels are to an automobile. Focus on sensation and surrender to lust before you start intercourse. Your sexual experience will be all play and no work. A couple that wants a meaningful sex life together needs to make a continual effort to court and romance each other. Communication is of upmost importance. Improving your sexual abilities and your emotional connection is the key to becoming the lover your lover wants.

NOTES

INTRODUCTION

1. Reay Tannahill, *Sex in History* (New York: Stein and Day, 1981), 160–61; Karla Baur and Robert Crooks, *Our Sexuality*, 11th ed. (Belmont, CA: Thomson Wadsworth, 2011), 10–12

2. Baur and Crooks, *Our Sexuality*, 408

I. WHAT INTERFERES WITH SEXUAL SUCCESS AND PLEASURE

1. Ellen Goodman, *Seattle Times* (July 19, 1996).

2. "Beaten Gay Student Dies: Murder Charges Planned," CNN.com (October 12, 1998).

3. Marty Klein, *America's War on Sex* (Westport, CT: Praeger Publishers, 2006), 11–13; Matt Apuzzo, "Abstinence Vows, Risk Taking Tied," Associated Press, Reuters.com (Saturday March 19, 2005).

4. Eric Berne, *Games People Play* (New York: Grove Press, 1964), 32–35.

5. *Webster's New Dictionary and Thesaurus* (Cleveland, OH: Wiley Publishing, 2002).

6. Karla Baur and Robert Crooks, *Our Sexuality*, 11th ed. (Belmont, CA: Thomson Wadsworth, 2008/2011), 11–12.

7. Jonathan Cott, *Isis and Osiris: Exploring the Goddess Myth* (New York: Doubleday, 1994), 27–31.

8. ibid.

9. ibid.

10. Genesis 3:1–24, The Holy Bible, Revised Standard Version (New York: Thomas Nelson & Sons, rev. 1952).

11. Reay Tannahill, *Sex in History* (New York, Stein and Day, 1982), 141–42; Baur and Crooks, *Our Sexuality*, 11–12.

12. Genesis 3:1–21, The Holy Bible, Revised Standard Version (New York: Thomas Nelson & Sons, rev. 1952).

13. Saint Thomas Aquinas, *Summa Theologica*, trans. Fathers of the English Dominican Province (New York: Bensinger Brothers Publishers, 1947).

14. Baur and Crooks, *Our Sexuality*, 11–12.

15. Cott, *Isis and Osiris*, 7–24.

16. Genesis 3:1–24.

17. Cott, *Isis and Osiris*, 7–24.

18. Genesis 3:1–24.

19. Baur and Crooks, *Our Sexuality*, 10–12.

20. J. Boswell, *Same Sex Unions in Pre-Modern Europe* (New York: Villard Publishing, 1994), 74; Ruth K. Westheimer and Sanford Lopater, *Human Sexuality* (Baltimore, MD: Lippincott Williams & Wilkins, 2005), 31–38.

21. Richard Bernstein, *The East, the West, and Sex* (New York: Alfred A. Knopf, 2009), 38–39.

22. ibid.

23. ibid.

24. Charles Freeman, *The Closing of the Western Mind* (New York: Vintage Books, 2005), 395–640; Tannahill, *Sex in History*, 141–42.

25. Baur and Crooks, *Our Sexuality*, 10–12.

26. Corinthians 7:1, The Holy Bible, Revised Standard Version (New York: Thomas Nelson & Sons, rev. 1952).

27. Baur and Crooks, 10–12.

28. ibid.

29. Baur and Crooks, *Our Sexuality*, 266.

30. ibid.

31. ibid.

32. Yahoo! search (2010), "Is Oral Sex Illegal in the United States?"

33. ibid., "Is Fornication Illegal in the United States?"

34. ibid., "Is Adultery Illegal in the United States?"

35. ibid., "Is Heterosexual Anal Sex Illegal in the United States?"

36. "Sodomy Laws in the United States: *Lawrence vs. Texas*," Wikipedia (2003).

37. Google search (2010). "Felony Sodomy Law Reinstated in Idaho."

38. "Facts on Sex Education in the United States," Guttmacher Institute.org (2006); "States Rejecting 'Abstinence-only' Funding," *CBS News*, Washington, January 7, 2008; Priya Alagiri, JD, Chris Collins, MPP, and Todd

Summers, "Abstinence Only vs. Comprehensive Sex Education" (Policy Monograph Series, March 2002).

39. Charles Freeman, *The Closing of the Western Mind* (New York: Vintage Books, 2005), 395–640; Baur and Crooks, *Our Sexuality*, 10–13.

40. "Galileo's Battle for the Heavens," *Nova*, Nova online home page (2002); Kathryn Kelly and Donn Byrne, *Exploring Human Sexuality* (Englewood Cliffs, NJ: Prentice-Hall, 1992), 15.

41. Sandra L. Caron, PhD, *Sex around the World: Cross-Culture Perspectives on Human Sexuality* (Boston: Pearson Custom Publishing, 2007), 125–28.

42. Richard Sipe, AW, *A Secret World: Sexuality and the Search for Celibacy* (New York: Brunner/Mazel, 1990).

43. Patrick Collinson, *The Reformation . . . A History* (Modern Library Edition, 2004), 178–82, www.modernlibrary.com.

44. Baur and Crooks, *Our Sexuality*, 12.

45. ibid.

46. Craig A. Hill, *Human Sexuality* (Thousand Oaks, CA: Sage Publications, 2008), 70–72; Edward L. Rowan, MD, *The Joy of Self-Pleasuring* (Amherst, NJ: Prometheus Books, 2000), 111–27; J. F. Kellogg, *Plain Facts for Old and Young* (Atlanta, GA: Segner & Company, 1891), 231–59; B. G. Jefferis and J. L. Nichols, *Safe Counsel* (Naperville, IL: J. L. Nichols & Company, 1922), 294–346, 438–40.

47. Baur and Crooks, *Our Sexuality*, 15.

48. ibid., 16.

49. Wardell B. Pomeroy, *Dr. Kinsey and the Institute for Sex Research* (New York: Harper & Row, 1972), 313, 333–34; Baur and Crooks, *Our Sexuality*, 408.

50. ibid.

51. Steven Watts, *Mr. Playboy: Hugh Hefner and the American Dream* (Hoboken, NJ: John Wiley & Sons, 2008), 64–65, 80.

52. Baur and Crooks, *Our Sexuality*, 40.

53. ibid., 555.

54. "Bush 'Disappointed' by Gay Marriage Ban's Defeat," CNN.com (July 15, 2004); Baur and Crooks, *Our Sexuality*, 25, 264, 283, 303, 323, 325, 485, 557.

2. THE NEGATIVE INFLUENCE OF THE BIBLE AND RELIGION ON OUR SEXUALITY

1. The Holy Bible, The Old Testament, Revised Standard Version (New York: Thomas Nelsen & Sons, rev. 1952).

2. ibid.

3. ibid.

4. ibid.

5. ibid.

6. ibid.

7. ibid.

8. ibid.

9. ibid.

10. ibid.

11. ibid.

12. The Holy Bible, The New Testament, Revised Standard Version (New York: Thomas Nelson & Sons, rev. 1952).

13. ibid.

14. ibid.

15. ibid.

16. ibid.

17. ibid.

18. ibid.

19. The Holy Bible, The New Testament.

20. Pope John Paul II, *Philadelphia Inquirer* (October 8, 1980), 3.

21. Robert Scheer "The *Playboy* Interview: Jimmy Carter" *Playboy*, col. 23, no. 11 (November 1976), 63–68.

22. The Holy Bible, The New Testament.

23. ibid.

24. ibid., Matthew 23:13–35.

25. ibid., Matthew 22:39; Mark 12:31.

3. THE IMPORTANCE OF EROTIC LANGUAGE IN MAKING LOVE

1. Karla Baur and Robert Crooks, *Our Sexuality*, 11th ed. (Belmont, CA: Thomson Wadsworth, 2008/2011), 12.

2. *Webster's New Dictionary and Thesaurus* (Cleveland, OH: Wiley Publishing Company, 2002).

3. Baur and Crooks, *Our Sexuality*, 40.

4. ibid., 164–68.

5. Murray S. Davis, *Smut: Erotic Reality/Obscene Ideology* (Chicago: The University of Chicago Press, 1983), 1–11.

6. Baur and Crooks, *Our Sexuality*, 164.

4. THE MECHANICS OF FEMALE ORGASM

1. Karla Baur and Robert Crooks, *Our Sexuality*, 11th ed. (Belmont, CA: Thomson Wadsworth, 2008/2011), 446.

2. Marc and Judith Meshorer, *Ultimate Pleasure: The Secrets of Easily Orgasmic Women* (New York: Saint Martin's Press, 1986), 25–35.

3. Sandra L. Caron, *Sex around the World* (Boston: Pearson Custom Publishing, 2007), 178–80.

4. ibid., 125–28.

5. Leora Tanenbaum, *Slut: Growing Up Female with a Bad Reputation* (New York: HarperCollins Publishers, 2000), 7–28, 37–40.

6. Barbara Ehrenreich, et al., *Re-making Love: The Feminization of Sex* (New York: Doubleday, 1987), 74–102; Baur and Crooks, *Our Sexuality*, 408.

7. Baur and Crooks, *Our Sexuality*, 29, 169.

8. Marie N. Robinson, MD, *The Power of Sexual Surrender* (New York: Doubleday, 1958), 58, ff.

9. ibid.

10. Arnold Kegel, MD, Lecture Seminar at The American Institute of Family Relations, Internship Training Program, Los Angeles, 1968.

11. ibid.

12. ibid.

13. ibid. B. Zilbergeld, *Male Sexuality: A Guide to Sexual Fulfillment* (Boston: Little Brown Publishers, 1978), 109.

14. Arnold Kegel, MD, Lecture Seminar.

15. Janell L. Carroll, *Sexuality Now* (Belmont, CA: Thomson Wadsworth, 2005), 292.

16. Masters and Johnson, Training Seminar in Sexual Dysfunction, Las Vegas, NV, October 4–5, 1977.

17. Ruth K. Westheimer and Sanford Lopater, *The G-Spot* (Baltimore, MD: Lippincott Williams & Wilkins, 2005), 241.

18. Baur and Crooks, *Our Sexuality*, 61, 169–70.

19. Masters and Johnson, Training Seminar.

20. Baur and Crooks, *Our Sexuality*, 10–12. Tanenbaum, *Slut: Growing Up Female with a Bad Reputation*, 7–28, 37–40.

5. SOLO SEX

1. Edward L Rowan, MD, *The Joy of Self-Pleasuring* (Amherst, NY: Prometheus Books, 2000), 102–3.

2. "Joycelyn Elders," Wikipedia, The Free Encyclopedia.

3. Rowan, 113.

4. ibid., 97.

5. ibid., 113–14.

6. ibid. Jean Stengers and Anne Van Neck, *Masturbation: The History of a Great Terror* (New York: Palgrave Press, 2001), 77–80.

7. B. G. Jefferis and J. L. Nichols, *Safe Counsel* (Naperville, IL: J. L. Nichols & Company, 1922), 294–346, 438–40.

8. Rowan, 114.

9. ibid., 118.

10. ibid., 118.

11. ibid., 120.

12. ibid., 122–23.

13. James H. Jones, *Alfred C. Kinsey: A Life* (New York: W. W. Norton & Company, 2004), 580–600.

14. Masters and Johnson, Training Seminar in Sexual Dysfunction, Las Vegas, NV, October 4–5, 1977.

15. "Prostate Massage and Health," Google.com.

16. Karla Baur and Robert Crooks, *Our Sexuality*, 11th ed. (Belmont, CA: Thomson Wadsworth, 2008/2011), 514. Anthony D'Amato, *Porn Up, Rape Down* (Northwestern Public Law Research Paper No. 913013, June 23, 2006, Northwestern University School of Law, Social Science Research Network).

17. Kristin Von Kreisler, "The Healing Powers of Sex," *Redbook*, April 1993.

18. ibid.

6. UNDERSTANDING MALE SEXUALITY

1. Dr. A. A. Brill, *The Basic Writings of Sigmund Freud* (New York, Random House, 1938), 592.

2. Chris Rock, "The Chris Rock Rule of Fidelity," *Laughing Man*, October 15, 2003.

3. Alfred C. Kinsey and Wardell B. Pomeroy, *Dr. Kinsey and the Institute for Sex Research* (New York: Harper & Row Publishers, 1972), 313, 333–34; Martin Weinberg, *Sex Research Studies from the Kinsey Institute* (New York: Oxford University Press, 1976), 60; Janell L. Carroll, *Sexuality Now* (Belmont, CA: Thomson Wadsworth, 2005), 291–92.

4. American Psychiatric Association, "DSM-5 Development" (Arlington, VA, 2010).

5. Patrick J. Carnes, PhD, and Stephanie Carnes, PhD, "Understanding Cybersex in 2010," *Family Therapy Magazine*, January/February 2010, 10–16.

6. Janell L. Carroll, *Sexuality Now* (Belmont, CA: Thomson Wadsworth, 2005), 519–20.

7. Janet Shibley Hyde and John D. Delamater, *Understanding Human Sexuality* (New York: McGraw-Hill, 2006), 404–5.

8. Patrick J. Carnes, PhD, and Stephanie Carnes, PhD, "Understanding Cybersex in 2010," *Family Therapy Magazine*, January/February 2010, 10–16.

9. ibid.

10. Marty Klein, PhD, *America's War on Sex: The Attack on Lust, Law, and Liberty* (Westport, CT: Praeger Publishers, 2006), 1–4.

11. Karla Baur and Robert Crooks, *Our Sexuality*, 11th ed. (Belmont, CA: Thomson Wadsworth, 2008/2011), 516.

12. Simon Louis Lajeunesse, PhD, "Pornography's Effect on Men Under Study" (University of Montreal, 2009), https://psychcentral.com.

13. ibid. Baur and Crooks, *Our Sexuality*, 558; Jerrold S. Greenberg, Clint E. Bruess, and C. Conklin, *Exploring the Dimensions of Human Sexuality*, 3rd ed. (Sudbury, MA: Jones and Bartlett Publishers, 2007), 764.

14. ibid., 554.

15. Jeffrey S. Nevid, Lois Fichner, and Spencer A. Rathus, *Human Sexuality in a World of Diversity*, 2nd ed. (Needham Heights, MA: Simon & Schuster, 1995), 635–42.

16. Nicholas, J. Karolides, Margaret Bald, and Dawn B. Sova, *100 Banned Books* (New York: Checkmark Books, 1999), 268–89.

17. Edward Donnerstein, Daniel Linz, and Steven Penrod, *The Question of Pornography: Research Findings, and Policy Implications* (New York: The Free Press, Macmillian, Inc., 1987), 61–66, 108–30; Liza Featherstone, "Porn," *Psychology Today*, September/October 2005; Lajeunesse, "Pornography's Effect"; The Society for the Scientific Study of Sexuality, "What Sexual Scientists Know about Pornography" (2005).

18. Baur and Crooks, *Our Sexuality*, 83.

19. Baur and Crooks, *Our Sexuality*, 159.

7. MARRIAGE

1. John, M. Gottman, PhD, *The Seven Principles of Making a Marriage Work* (New York: Three Rivers Press, 1999), 102–3.

2. Ministry of Integration and Gender Equality, *Equal Rights and Opportunities Regardless of Sexual Orientation or Transgender Identity or Expres-*

sion (Government Office of Sweden, October 2009). Katrin Bennhold, "The Female Factor: Men Can Have It All," *New York Times*, June 9, 2010.

3. Sandra Caron, PhD, *Sex around the World: Cross-Culture Perspectives on Human Sexuality* (Boston: Pearson Custom Publishing, 2007), 177. "Prostitution in Sweden," Wikipedia.org (2010).

4. "Women Prime Ministers and Presidents, Heads of State: 20th century," About.com., Women's History.

5. Amy Joyce, "Women Severely Underrepresented in Fortune 500 Companies," *Washington Post*, August 6, 2006.

6. Sandra L. Caron, *Sex around the World: Cross-Culture Perspectives on Human Sexuality* (Boston: Pearson Custom Publishing, 2007).

7. ibid.

8. Gottman, *The Seven Principles*, 103.

9. CONCLUSION

1. Associated Press, February 20, 2010.

2. Sandra L. Caron, *Sex around the World: Cross-Culture Perspectives on Human Sexuality* (Boston: Pearson Custom Publishing, 2007), 125.

3. Caron, *Sex around the World*, 177–202, 207.

4. Karla Baur and Robert Crooks, *Our Sexuality*, 11th ed. (Belmont, CA: Thomson Wadsworth, 2008/2011), 8.

5. Donald Marshall, "Too Much in Mangaia," *Psychology Today*, February 1971.

6. ibid.

7. ibid.

8. Marty Klein, *America's War on Sex* (Westport, CT: Praeger Publishers, 2006), 5–18.

9. Carissa Wolf, "The Forgotten Epidemic," *Idaho Statesman*, November 25, 2009.

10. Baur and Crooks, *Our Sexuality*, 380.

11. Alison Flood, "Sherman Alexie Young Adult Book Banned in Idaho Schools," *The Guardian*, April 8, 2014.

12. Patrick Malone and Monica Rodriguez, *Comprehensive Sex Education vs. Abstinence-Only-Until-Marriage Program*, vol. 38, no. 2 (Sexuality Information and Educational Council of the United States, 2016).

13. Klein, *America's War on Sex*, 13–17, 206.

14. Baur and Crooks, *Our Sexuality*, 381–85.

15. Masters and Johnson, Training Seminar in Sexual Dysfunction, Las Vegas, NV, October 4–5, 1977.

16. Janell L. Carroll, *Sexuality Now*, 3rd ed. (Belmont, CA: Thomson Wadsworth, 2010), 273.

17. Baur and Crooks, *Our Sexuality*, 422.

REFERENCES

Alagiri, Priya, JD, Chris Collins, MPP, and Todd Summers. *Abstinence Only vs. Comprehensive Sex Education*. Policy Monograph Series, March 2002.

American Psychiatric Association. "DSM-5 Development." Arlington, VA: 2010.

Apuzzo, Matt. *Abstinence Vows, Risk Taking Tied*. Reuters.com. Associated Press (March 19, 2005).

Aquinas, Saint Thomas. *Summa Theologica*. Translated by the Fathers of the English Dominican Province. New York: Bensinger Brothers, 1947.

Associated Press (February 20, 2010).

Baur, Karla, and Robert Crooks. *Our Sexuality*. 11th ed. Belmont, CA: Thomson Wadsworth, 2008/2011.

"Beaten Gay Student Dies: Murder Charges Planned." CNN.com (October 12, 1998).

Bennhold, Katrin. "The Female Factor: Men Can Have It All." *New York Times* (June 9, 2010).

Berne, Eric. *Games People Play*. New York: Grove Press, 1964.

Bernstein, Richard. *The East, the West, and Sex*. New York: Alfred A. Knopf, 2009.

Boswell, J. *Same Sex Unions in Pre-Modern Europe*. New York: Villard Publishing, 1994.

Brill, A. A., Dr. *The Basic Writings of Sigmund Freud*. New York: Random House, 1938.

"Bush 'Disappointed' by Gay Marriage Ban's Defeat." CNN.com (July 15, 2004).

Carnes, Patrick J., PhD, and Stephanie Carnes, PhD. "Understanding Cybersex in 2010." *Family Therapy Magazine* (January/February 2010).

Caron, Sandra L., PhD. *Sex around the World: Cross-Culture Perspectives on Human Sexuality*. Boston: Pearson Custom Publishing, 2007.

Carroll, Janell, L. *Sexuality Now*. Belmont, CA: Thomson Wadsworth, 2005.

Collinson, Patrick. *The Reformation . . . A History*. Modern Library Edition, 2004. www.modernlibrary.com.

Cott, Jonathan. *Isis and Osiris: Exploring the Goddess Myth*. New York: Doubleday, 1994.

D'Amato, Anthony. *Porn Up, Rape Down*. Northwestern Public Law Research Paper No. 913013 (June 23, 2006). Northwestern University-School of Law. Social Science Research Network.

Davis, Murray S. *Smut: Erotic Reality/Obscene Ideology*. Chicago: The University of Chicago Press, 1983.

Donnerstein, Edward, Daniel Linz, and Steven Penrod. *The Question of Pornography: Research Findings, and Policy Implications*. New York: The Free Press, Macmillan Publishers, 1987.

Ehrenreich, Barbara, et al. *Re-making Love: The Feminization of Sex*. New York: Doubleday, 1987.

"Facts on Sex Education in the United States." GuttmacherInstitute.org (2006).

Featherstone, Liza. "Porn." *Psychology Today* (September/October 2005).

Flood, Alison. "Sherman Alexie Young Adult Book Banned in Idaho Schools." *The Guardian* (April 8, 2014).

Freeman, Charles. *The Closing of the Western Mind*. New York: Vintage Books, 2005.

"Galileo's Battle for the Heavens." *Nova*. Nova online home page (2002).

Goodman, Ellen. *Seattle Times* (July 19, 1996).

Google search (2010). "Felony Sodomy Law Reinstated in Idaho."

Gottman, John M., PhD. *The Seven Principles of Making a Marriage Work*. New York: Three Rivers Press, 1999.

Greenberg, Jerrold S., Clint E. Bruess, and C. Conklin. *Exploring the Dimensions of Human Sexuality*. 3rd ed. Sudbury, MA: Jones and Bartlett Publishers, 2007.

Hill, Craig A. *Human Sexuality*. Thousand Oaks, CA: Sage Publications, 2008.

Hyde, Janet Shibley, and John D. Delamater. *Understanding Human Sexuality*. New York: McGraw-Hill, 2006.

Jefferis, B. G., and J. L. Nichols. *Safe Counsel*. Naperville, IL: J. L. Nichols & Company, 1922.

Jones, James H. *Alfred C. Kinsey: A Life*. New York: W. W. Norton & Company, 2004.

Joyce, Amy. "Women Severely Underrepresented in Fortune 500 Companies." *Washington Post* (August 6, 2006).

"Jocelyn Elders." Wikipedia, The Free Encyclopedia.

Karolides, Nicholas J., Margaret Bald, and Dawn B. Sova. *100 Banned Books: Censorship Histories of World Literature*. New York: Checkmark Books, 1999.

Kegel, Arnold, MD. Lecture Seminar. Intern Training Program. American Institute of Family Relations. Los Angeles, 1968.

Kellogg, J. F. *Plain Facts for Old and Young*. Atlanta, GA: Segner & Company, 1891.

Kelly, Kathryn, and Donn Byrne. *Exploring Human Sexuality*. Englewood Cliffs, NJ: Prentice-Hall, 1992.

Kinsey, Alfred C., and Wardell B. Pomeroy. *Dr. Kinsey and the Institute for Sex Research*. New York: Harper & Row Publishers, 1972.

Klein, Marty. *America's War on Sex*. Westport, CT: Praeger Publishers, 2006.

Kreisler, Kristin Von. "The Healing Powers of Sex." *Redbook* (April 1993).

Lajeunesse, Simon Louis, PhD. *Pornography's Effect on Men under Study*. University of Montreal, 2009. https://psychcentral.com.

Malone, Patrick, and Monica Rodriguez. *Comprehensive Sex Education vs. Abstinence-Only-Until-Marriage Program*. vol. 38. no. 2. Sexuality Information and Educational Council of the United States, 2016.

Marshall, Donald. "Too Much in Mangaia." *Psychology Today* (February 1971).

Masters and Johnson. Training Seminar in Sexual Dysfunction. Las Vegas, NV, October 4–5, 1977.

Meshorer, Marc and Judith. *Ultimate Pleasure: The Secrets of Easily Orgasmic Women*. New York: Saint Martin's Press, 1986.

Ministry of Integration and Gender Equality. *Equal Rights and Opportunities Regardless of Sexual Orientation or Transgender Identity or Expression*. Government Office of Sweden Publication, October 2009.

Nevid, Jeffery S., Lois Fichner, and Spencer A. Rathus. *Human Sexuality in a World of Diversity*. 2nd ed. Needham Heights, MA: Simon & Schuster Company, 1995.

Pomeroy, Wardell B. *Dr. Kinsey and the Institute for Sex Research*. New York: Harper & Row, 1972.

Pope John Paul II, *Philadelphia Inquirer* (October 8, 1980): 3.

"Prostate Massage and Health." Google.com.

"Prostitution in Sweden." Wikipedia.org (2010).

Robinson, Marie N., MD. *The Power of Sexual Surrender*. New York: Doubleday, 1958.

Rock, Chris. "The Chris Rock Rule of Fidelity." *Laughing Man*, October 15, 2003.

Rowan, Edward L., MD. *The Joy of Self-Pleasuring*. Amherst, NJ: Prometheus Books, 2000.

Scheer, Robert. "The Playboy Interview: Jimmy Carter." *Playboy*, vol. 23, no. 11 (November 1976).

Sipe, Richard, AW. *A Secret World: Sexuality and the Search for Celibacy*. New York: Brunner/Mazel, 1990.

"Sodomy Laws in the United States: Lawrence vs. Texas." Wikipedia (2003).

"States Rejecting 'Abstinence-only' Funding." *CBS News*. Washington (January 7, 2008).

Stengers, Jean, and Anne Van Neck. *Masturbation: The History of a Great Terror*. New York: Palgrave Press, 2001.

Tanenbaum, Leora. *Slut: Growing Up Female with a Bad Reputation*. New York: Harper-Collins Publishers, 2000.

Tannahill, Reay. *Sex in History*. New York: Stein and Day, 1981.

The Holy Bible. Revised Standard Version. New York: Thomas Nelson & Sons, rev. 1952.

The Society for the Scientific Study of Sexuality. "What Sexual Scientists Know about Pornography." 2005.

Watts, Steven. *Mr. Playboy: Hugh Hefner and the American Dream*. Hoboken, NJ: John Wiley & Sons, 2008.

Webster's New Dictionary and Thesaurus. Cleveland, OH: Wiley Publishing, 2002.

Weinberg, Martin. *Sex Research Studies from the Kinsey Institute*. New York: Oxford University Press, 1976.

Westheimer, Ruth K., and Sanford Lopater. *Human Sexuality*. Baltimore, MD: Lippincott Williams & Wilkins, 2005.

———. *The G-Spot*. Baltimore, MD: Lippincott Williams & Wilkins, 2005.

Wolf, Carissa. "The Forgotten Epidemic." *Idaho Statesman* (November 25, 2009).

"Women Prime Ministers and Presidents, Heads of State: 20th Century." About.com. Women's History.

Yahoo! search (2010). "Is Oral Sex Illegal in the United States?"

———. "Is Adultery Illegal in the United States?"

———. "Is Fornication Illegal in the United States?"

———. "Is Heterosexual Anal Sex Illegal in the United States?"

Zilbergeld, B. *Male Sexuality: A Guide to Sexual Fulfillment*. Boston: Little Brown Publishers, 1978.

INDEX

abortion, 11, 12, 24, 73, 125–126, 127, 129. *See also* contraception; morning after pill

abstinence: abstinence sex education, 2, 11, 15, 44, 125, 127, 129, 130; abstinence until marriage, 2, 5, 8, 9, 10, 15, 17, 23, 24, 44, 60, 105, 126, 127, 130; in politics, 127; in Christianity, 7

Acton, William, 13

adultery, 8, 25–26

AIDS, 17

Alexie, Sherman, 129

antioxidants, 55, 64

arthritis, 64

Barbach, Lonnie, 92

Bekker, Balthazar, 57. *See also* onanism.

Berne, Eric, 2

birth control, 8, 9, 17, 24, 56, 62, 125–126, 127, 130; coitus interruptus, 56. *See also* contraception.

Boise State University, 128

book banning/burning, 13, 129

Bush, George W., 17

Carnes, Patrick, 73

Carter, James (Jimmy), 26, 28

Christianity, 6, 7, 9, 11, 12, 15, 24, 55, 56, 73; Adam and Eve, 3, 4, 5, 7, 45, 51, 52; Saint Augustine, 3, 4, 7, 8, 33, 51;

baptism, 7; celibacy, 7, 8, 12, 23, 29; Saint Christopher, 70; Emperor Constantine, 7; Eve, 33, 45, 80, 89; Garden of Eden, 4, 5, 51; Genesis, 3, 4, 5, 7, 56; homosexuality, 9, 10, 17, 20, 22, 24; Jesus, 7, 25, 26, 27, 28, 30; Luther, Martin, 12; Mary, 5, 7, 45; Matthew, 25, 26, 27, 76; Mormon, 10, 73; New Testament, 22–24, 29, 45; Old Testament, 3, 4, 20–22, 29, 30, 56; Onan, 56; original sin, 7; Saint Paul, 3, 7, 8, 24, 33, 51; Pope John Paul II, 25, 55; pro-choice/pro-life, 12, 17; procreation, 7, 8, 9, 12; Protestant, 9, 11, 12, 25, 55; Protestant Reformation, 12, 17; Puritan, 11; Roman Catholic Church/Catholicism, 3, 4, 7, 8–9, 10, 11, 12, 25, 29, 31, 55, 57, 70, 73, 88; Satan, 4; sex in marriage, 9; sin, 2, 4, 5, 7–8, 9, 12, 13, 14, 15, 25, 26, 28, 29, 31, 32, 33, 55, 71, 73, 76, 77, 134; Ten Commandments, 27, 28; Saint Thomas Aquinas, 3, 5, 8, 33, 51, 134; Tree of Knowledge, 4. *See also* gay rights and marriage; religion.

Clinton, William (Bill), 55; Elder, Jocelyn, 55

clitoris, 29, 44, 45, 47, 48, 51, 58, 126, 127, 134

communication, 86, 104, 107, 121, 122; defensive response, 87; empathy, 104;

erotic, 33; language of endearment, 102, 107, 109, 111, 112–113, 122, 139; rules, 90; unresponsive/silent treatment, 86, 87

comprehensive sex education, 10, 11, 17, 42, 44, 48, 73, 76, 125–126, 126, 127, 129, 130; Planned Parenthood, 105, 129, 130

compulsive sexual behavior. *See* sexual addiction

connecting and disconnecting, 97, 101; emotional and psychological connections/intimacy, 42, 54, 70, 81, 84, 97, 98, 101, 102, 106, 107, 111, 114, 119, 120, 123, 124, 139

contact time/rituals, 96, 97, 106, 107; *See also* marriage, dating within.

contraception, 11, 14, 73, 130, 131; birth control pill, 16; condom, 11, 128; morning after pill, 73, 126, 127

Crimes against Nature, 3, 8, 9. *See also* Crimes against Nature criminal law; fornication law.

Davis, Murray S., 34

deep erotic state, 29, 33, 36, 47, 55, 64, 133, 134, 139

divorce, 68, 87, 114, 118, 120, 121, 123

Ellis, Havelock, 58

Emmet, Idaho, 1

emotional love, 84, 85, 96, 110

endorphins, 55, 64

erection, 25, 29, 35, 42, 58, 62, 69, 81, 98, 133, 136, 138; erection drugs, 81, 82, 102, 137, 139

erogenous zones, 34, 48–49, 50, 126, 139

erotic reality, 34, 35, 36, 39, 49, 60, 78, 137. *See also* everyday reality.

everyday reality, 34, 36. *See also* erotic reality.

female: gender discrimination, 43; menstruation, 15, 55, 63, 69, 90; right to vote, 14; in the workforce, 15; submission, 24

foreplay, 8, 29, 32, 34, 41, 49, 78, 82, 134, 138–139

fornication law, 10; Idaho, 1; US Supreme Court, 10

Freud, Sigmund, 45, 46, 58, 68

G-spot, 41, 50, 83

Galileo, 11

Gallup poll, 9

Garden of Conventional Thinking, 52. *See also* Garden of Eden.

gay rights and marriage, 17, 20, 73, 127

Gottman, John, 90

Gräfenberg, Ernst, 50

Graham, Sylvester, 58; graham cracker, 58

Great Depression, 14, 17

headache, 55, 64

Hefner, Hugh, 16, 129

"hoodwinked", 130, 136

immune system, 55, 57, 64

incest, 8

infidelity, 16, 80, 115, 117–118, 118–119, 120, 121; prevention of, 114, 121–123. *See also* marriage, affair; monogamy.

integrity, 115, 117, 123

Jefferis, B.G., 57

Kegel, Arnold, 46, 47, 48. *See also* pubococcygeus muscle.

Kegel squeezes, 47, 48. *See also* Kegel, Arnold.

Kellogg, J.F., 58; Corn Flakes, 58

Kinsey, Alfred, PhD, 15, 16, 59, 72, 129; Kinsey Institute, 114

Klein, Martin (Marty), 73. *See also* scripting; erotophobe.

lust, 29, 32, 34, 49, 50, 60, 76, 77, 80, 93, 135

Madonna-Whore Complex, 32. *See also* Mary versus Eve.

making erotica, 33

Mangaia, 43, 126–127; Marshall, Donald S., 126

marriage: affair, 72, 85, 102, 113, 114, 115, 117–118, 119–120, 120;

communication, 70, 86, 99, 120, 121, 134, 139; counseling, 123, 128; dating within, 95; dissatisfaction within, 90, 119; emotional commitment, 123; independence, 103, 104; mental illness, 123; open marriage, 114; sex outside of, 15, 17, 32, 44; sexual exclusivity, 70, 123, 135; sexual frustration within, 131, 134, 138

Mary versus Eve, 5, 32. *See also* Christianity; religion

Masters and Johnson, 16, 34, 36, 47, 48–49, 50, 55, 61, 63, 98, 129, 133, 137, 138; The Four Phase Sexual Response Cycle, 34, 35

masturbation/self-sex/solo sex, 11, 13, 14, 15, 17, 42, 44, 45, 48, 49, 50, 54, 55, 57, 58–59, 59–64, 69, 72, 73, 81, 92, 102, 105, 128, 129, 131, 135, 137; "onanism", 57, 59; premarital, 63, 73; in religion, 3, 4, 8, 9, 24, 55, 56; self-abuse, 57, 58

Meese, Edwin, 17, 75; Meese Commission Report, 75

Meridian, Idaho: Meridian School District, 128, 129

Middle Ages, 3, 8, 9, 11, 45, 55. *See also* scripting, Middle Ages.

Middle East, 80

monogamy, 70, 114, 115, 123; "new monogamy", 114. *See also* infidelity; marriage; sexual exclusivity.

monster moralists, 33

National Health and Social Life Survey, 114

orgasm, 14, 15, 29, 31, 32, 34, 35, 36, 41, 42, 43, 45, 45–46, 47, 48–49, 50, 55, 58, 59, 60, 61, 62, 63, 63–64, 77, 78, 80, 81, 83, 92, 93, 126, 127, 128, 131, 133, 134, 135, 136, 137, 138; faking orgasm, 41, 42, 43, 63, 92; female hormonal issues, 43; frigidity, 45; orgasmic platform, 47; pelvic contractions, 43, 48; "pre-orgasmic", 45, 48

parent ego state, 32

pelvic congestion, 55, 63

penis, 9, 29, 31, 45, 48, 76, 82, 83, 131; amulet, 6, 70; Cowper's gland, 131

Pomeroy, Wardell, 129

pornography, 13, 17, 44, 63, 71, 71–72, 73–76, 76–77, 77–79, 79–80, 80, 81, 85, 86, 98, 102, 133, 134–135, 137; Bruce, Lenny, 72; erotic video/material, 50, 77, 79, 81; in marriage, 67, 69, 70, 78; internet pornography, 75; Lajeunesse, Simon Louis, 75; Kama Sutra, 70; Schunga, 70; Stewart, Potter, 71; women's pornography, 79

premarital sex, 5, 73

prostate, 61, 69

prostitution, 88, 89, 125; American, 89; ancient Greece, 6

public/private self, 111

pubococcygeus muscle, 46, 47, 48

rape, 8, 63, 68, 75, 80

religion, 2; Divine Mother, 7; Egyptian, 3–4, 5, 6–7, 12, 17, 55; Greek, 6–7, 12, 17; Judaism, 2, 4, 9, 27, 29, 56, 73; Muslim, 2, 9, 73; Roman, 6, 7, 12, 17, 70. *See also* Christianity.

Reagan, Ronald, 17, 75

Renaissance, 12, 17

Roaring Twenties, 14, 17

Robinson, Marie, 46

Rock, Chris, 69, 114

Rush, Benjamin, 57

"scripting," 2, 3, 5, 12, 17, 131; American, 7, 8, 17, 26, 43, 70, 80, 87, 88, 114, 115, 126, 127, 129, 130, 131, 133, 136; erotophobe, 52, 73, 74, 130, 136; medical, 14; Middle Ages, 131; negative scripting, 2, 3, 12, 15, 16, 28, 31, 32, 33, 43, 45, 48, 50, 52, 54, 55, 71, 73, 74, 77, 79, 80, 85, 88, 92, 93, 99, 104, 110, 127, 130, 133, 135, 136, 138; positive scripting, 5, 12, 14, 15; Puritan, 71, 76, 88; religious, 8, 10, 16, 28, 51; Victorian, 13, 71, 76, 88, 94

sexual addiction, 28, 72, 73; Carnes, Patrick, PhD, 73; mental illness, 73; movement, 72, 73

sexual dysfunction, 29, 34, 46, 63, 82

sexual harassment, 68; narcissism, 68
Sexuality Information and Education
    Council, 129
sexuality: Christian, 131; male, 67, 101.
    See also religion.
sexual segregation, 13
sexual tension, 33–34, 35, 36, 43, 47, 48,
    49, 54, 60, 63, 65, 66, 69, 78, 81, 83,
    90, 94, 101, 102, 121, 136
sexually transmitted disease, 16, 63, 128,
    129. *See also* AIDS.
SIE-CUS. *See* Sexuality Information and
    Education Council
social sex, 54, 61, 62, 63, 64
sphincter, 47, 48

testosterone, 68, 83, 90
Tissot, Samuel David, 57

United States: Crimes against Nature
    criminal law, 8; gay marriage, 129;
    government, 2; rape, 75; Supreme
    Court, 129

vagina, 31, 35, 47, 48, 50, 82, 83; cervix,
    82; vaginal orgasm, 45, 46, 47
vasocongestion, 55, 63
Victoria, Queen, 13
Victorian era, 12–13, 13, 14, 17, 45; "neo-
    Victorian", 17, 73
virginity, 5, 44, 45, 63, 125

Washington, George, 57. *See also* Rush,
    Benjamin.
Webster's Dictionary, 130
Western civilization, 3, 7, 11, 17, 45
Whipple, Beverly and Perry, John, 50, 64.
    See also G-spot
World War II, 15, 17

ABOUT THE AUTHOR

Frederick D. Mondin, EdD, has counseled thousands of individuals and couples. His private practice as a marriage and sexuality counselor spans more than four decades, and he also was an adjunct professor in human sexuality at Boise State University for twenty-five years.

Prior to becoming a therapist, Frederick Mondin was ordained as a Presbyterian minister in 1965. When Dr. Mondin married Dr. Joan Henderson in 1976 they merged their practices, providing a complete range of counseling and psychology services

Mondin is a clinical member of the American Association of Marriage and Family Therapists, a licensed Marriage and Family Therapist, and a licensed Clinical Professional Counselor. In addition, he is also a member of the Sexuality Information and Education Council of the United States and the American Association of Sexuality Educators, Counselors, and Therapists. He and his wife reside in the mountains, just outside of Boise, Idaho.